HOW TO BECOME
A PROBATION OFFICER

D1354000

www.How2Become.com

Orders: Please contact How2become Ltd, Suite 2, 50 Churchill Square Business Centre, Kings Hill, Kent ME19 4YU.

You can order through Amazon.co.uk under ISBN 978-1-910602-44-7, via the website www.How2Become.com or through Gardners.com.

ISBN: 978-1-910602-44-7

First published in 2015 by How2become Ltd.

Typeset for How2become Ltd by Anton Pshinka.

Disclaimer

Every effort has been made to ensure that the information contained within this guide is accurate at the time of publication. How2become Ltd are not responsible for anyone failing any part of any selection process as a result of the information contained within this guide. How2become Ltd and their authors cannot accept any responsibility for any errors or omissions within this guide, however caused. No responsibility for loss or damage occasioned by any person acting, or refraining from action, as a result of the material in this publication can be accepted by How2become Ltd.

The information within this guide does not represent the views of any third party service or organisation.

CONTENTS

INTRODUCTION

Do you sit there dreaming about performing heroic actions, or of dramatically saving the day? You are not alone. Unfortunately, there are millions of people who would rather watch their heroes on TV, than take direct action. These people will tell you that superheroes are a product of fiction, and that they don't exist.

Well, it might shock you to learn that there are real life heroes walking amongst us every day. These people spend their whole lives assisting others. They help the most vulnerable members of society get back on their feet. They serve in prisons, community homes and detention centres. They work around the clock, to make sure that every single citizen is treated fairly, despite their circumstances. They don't have a cape, and they certainly can't fly, but what they can do is make a difference. Who are these people we are referring to? They are Probation Officers. The great news is, YOU can become one of them!

The topics that we will cover include:

- The daily requirements of a Probation Officer;

- The core competencies needed for the job role;

- The qualifications, training and experience needed;

- The role of a PSO (Probation Services Officer);

- The role of a PO (Probation Officer) and how to progress to this point;

- Detailed interview advice, including sample questions and answers;

- Real day in the life segments of experienced professionals within the field.

This professional guide is for anyone who is serious about becoming a Probation Officer. This book will guide you through the step-by-step process of becoming a Proba-tion Officer and teach you ways to better your chances of success!

The road to becoming a Probation Officer is long and difficult. You will be pushed to your limits by the situations that you will encounter, and by the people that you will meet. What you need to remember is that all of this will make you stronger, more experienced and ultimately more suitable for the job role.

With the help of our guide, you can prepare yourself for the process. How2Become will be with you on every step of the journey. Using this book, you can secure your dream job, and start making a difference to others people's lives.

Believe in yourself, and you can achieve anything that you set your mind to.

CHAPTER 1

The Role
of a Probation
Officer

The role of a Probation Officer is primarily to deal with individuals who are currently serving, or have previously served, prison or community sentences. Sometimes, you will also work with these individuals before they are even sentenced.

The aim of a Probation Officer is to:

- Ensure that offenders carry out their punishment in a problem-free manner;

- Help offenders who have been released make a smooth transition back into the community;

- Educate offenders on how their crimes have impacted both their victims and the general public.

For some people, this might sound intimidating. The thought of working with (sometimes hardened) criminals is particularly daunting. Throughout this guide, you will find a number of sample exercises, which will test you on-the-spot in regards to a particular situation. These will provide you with initial and theoretical experience in dealing with some of the situations that you might encounter whilst working as a Probation Officer. Crucially, these exercises will also test you on the core competencies required for the role.

PROBATION OFFICER CORE COMPETENCIES

Core competencies refer to the key behaviours which you will be expected to demonstrate whilst a) applying for a job position and b) working within the role. Core competencies are an integral part of any job selection process, and are now used by almost every single employer.

In order to successfully hold down a position as a Probation Officer, you will need to show an ability to demonstrate these core competencies at all times. These competencies are important because they benefit both the safety of the officer and the safety of the individual that they are dealing with.

Below, we will list all of the Probation Officer core competencies, which you should be aware of:

Communication:

As a Probation Officer, your **communicational ability** will be your biggest and most important tool. There is arguably no attribute that is more essential to the role of a Probation Officer than good communication.

The majority of your working hours will be spent dealing with extremely difficult individuals, many of whom will be uncooperative. You'll have to demonstrate extensive powers of persuasion and negotiation in order to convince these individuals to agree with your proposed course of action, and there will be times when they simply refuse to listen to you altogether. In these cases, you'll have to be incredibly patient and understanding.

Although you might feel it, you must never show anger or frustration towards offenders. There will be times when you must be stern, and you will more than likely have to make decisions that you don't necessarily agree with, but you must always be polite and respectful no matter who you are dealing with. Working as a Probation Officer will bring you into contact with:

- Law enforcement;
- Courts;
- Legal teams;
- Welfare officers;
- Counsellors;
- Medical staff.

You will need to communicate with all of the aforementioned in order to agree on a suitable course of action. You will often find yourself negotiating with these people on behalf of the offenders that you are working with, in order to explain the situation or prevent action being taken against the offender.

Respect for Others:

As mentioned, when working as a Probation Officer you will need to demonstrate a **respect for others** at all times. It is extremely important that you aren't judgemental, and treat every person that you work with as fairly as possible.

There will be many occasions when you find yourself working with people whom you don't necessarily get on with. It's crucial that you don't go into these meetings with preconceived ideas.

Remember that your goal is to help offenders, not judge them. The best way to do this is treat every case with an open mind. An understanding of diversity also falls under this competency. There may be times when you have to deal with ethnic offenders, or even racial issues that have arisen with other offenders.

It's vital that you have the necessary understanding to deal with these problems. If you cannot display a respect for diversity, then you are highly unlikely to even pass the application stage of the process.

Risk Assessment:

Probation Officers need to demonstrate the core competency of **risk assessment** on a daily basis. This will be absolutely crucial when making a decision regarding offenders. You will need to show that you have given consideration for both their own and public safety.

As we have mentioned, sometimes you might have to make decisions that you don't necessarily like. For example, if you feel that an offender with whom you have built up a relationship would be better served in custody, then it is your responsibility to make this happen.

You'll also need to perform risk assessment based on what exterior services to include i.e. if an offender needs to be referred to a specialist psychiatric team. In every single case that you work on, you will need to carefully balance the pros and cons in order to come to safe and informed decisions, which will benefit both the offender and the general public.

UK based Probation Officers have a particular system in place, which determines how they perform risk assessment. This is known as *'OASys' (Offender Assessment System).*

OASys helps Probation Officers to:

- Assess how likely an individual is to re-offend;

- Assess whether an individual is at risk of serious harm, and whether they pose a risk to others;

- Assess the need to include further exterior specialists;

- Assess levels of behavioural change in an individual.

Adaptability:

When working as a Probation Officer, you will often come across times when you need to **adapt** your thought process or prioritise according to the situation that you are in.

For example, if you are working on two separate cases, and one offender suddenly gets themselves into trouble, you will have to act quickly and decisively in order to solve this issue. You'll need to prioritise which cases are the most important, and come up with creative and logical solutions to problems.

Remember that every single case will be different, individuals will test you in a variety of ways and you will need to be prepared to deal with all of these. Therefore, an ability to adapt your thinking and be flexible with solutions is essential.

Teamwork:

While you will not necessarily be working as part of a team directly, as a Probation Officer you will **work as part of a wider unit**. You'll have to work in conjunction with law enforcement, medical staff, voluntary workers, counsellors and legal teams, in order to provide the best possible service for offenders.

As we have already outlined, this means you'll need to be a competent communicator, and must be able to get along with all different types of people. Working as part of a team means being able to negotiate, organise and come to agreements with other members of your team.

As a wider unit, you will be responsible for making sure that the offender is successfully rehabilitated and transitions as smoothly as possible back into society, or even into prison. If every member of the team does their job to the best of their ability, then the job is accomplished far easier.

As a Probation Officer, you must have an ability to: identify legislation, organisational policies and procedures which relate to working as a member of a team. You will also need to demonstrate an understanding of how legislation, policies and procedures can affect your working relationship with other/outside agencies. To add to this, you must be able to identify the particular roles and functions of these agencies in the sector and in relation to your case. Finally, you'll need to be able to describe how you can use different methods of communication to deal with different agencies, and explain the core principles of joint-working.

Case Management:

This is a very specific competency, and refers more to the general overview of a Probation Officer's work. As a Probation Officer, you'll have to work directly with offenders, with the aim of preparing them for time in prison, helping them cope in prison, or rehabilitating them after prison.

Collectively, this is known as **case management**. It incorporates all of the previously listed competencies, and also involves skills such as developing proposals, writing reports, assessing individual needs, planning activities and organising interventions. Report writing and proposal development are particularly important. In this guide, we will provide you with multiple practice exercises to not only better your management skills, but all of the other core competencies required.

In the following chapter, we have included sample exercises linking to each of the core competencies as listed above.

CHAPTER 2

*Core Competency
Sample
Exercises*

Communication Exercise

You are a Probation Officer working with a recently paroled offender. Joe was in prison for 8 months, for committing perjury. He is a compulsive liar and often exaggerates wildly for effect. In the past, you have had trouble when meeting with Joe on a one-to-one basis, as it is often difficult to ascertain the truth behind what he is saying.

You were due to meet Joe at 10am this morning. He did not show up, but you have received a text message from him claiming that he is somewhere in the middle of East-Ham, after being caught up in a fight at a local pub. He describes the scene as 'all kicking off' and claims that 'he dodged two men tackling each other'.

To your knowledge, Joe lives several hours from this location. There have been no police reports of a fight in this area.

Look at the below options, and order the responses into most effective, least effective and ineffective.

	Most Effective	Least Effective	Ineffective
Thank Joe, and let him know that you'll see him next week.			
Tell Joe that you are furious about his failure to attend, and will not be seeing him again.			
Ask Joe to meet you as soon as possible, in order to discuss why he failed to turn up.			

How to answer this question:

The most effective way to respond to Joe would be to *"ask him to meet you as soon as possible, in order to discuss why he failed to turn up"*.

• You need to get to the bottom of the incident, especially since he claims to have been involved in a fight. This could damage his parole status.

The least effective way to respond to Joe would be to *"tell him that you are furious about his failure to attend, and that you will not be seeing him again"*.

• As his Probation Officer, you are responsible for monitoring and amending his behaviour. By refusing to see him, you would be acting in direct contrast to your duties. You also need to remain calm, composed and understanding at all times.

The ineffective way to respond to Joe would be to *"thank him, and let him know that you'll see him next week"*.

• This does nothing to solve the issue, and will make him think that missing meetings is acceptable.

Respect for Others Exercise

In this exercise, you are a customer services officer working for a shopping centre. A woman has come to see you with a complaint. She is not happy about the number of ethnic shoppers at the venue, and believes that there should be a limit to how many foreign people are let into the building. The woman is extremely angry, and starts to become verbally abusive towards you.

Look at the below options, and order the responses into most effective, least effective and ineffective.

	Most Effective	Least Effective	Ineffective
Tell the woman that you have taken her request into consideration, and will look into making the requested changes.			
Tell the woman that this centre has a fairness and equality policy, which her request is in direct violation of, and that she is free to shop elsewhere if she doesn't like that.			
Tell the woman that her request is in direct violation of the fairness and equality policy, and that this centre promotes and welcomes people of all backgrounds. Call security to escort her from the building.			

How to answer this question:

The most effective way to respond to this would be to *"tell the woman that her request is in direct violation of the fairness and equality policy, and then call security"*.

• The fact that she has been verbally abusive means that she is no longer welcome on the premises.

The least effective way to respond to this would be to *"tell the woman that you will look into making the requested changes"*.

• You need to demonstrate that you will not tolerate discrimination of any kind.

The ineffective way to respond to this would be to *"tell the woman that she is free to shop elsewhere if she doesn't like it"*.

• Not only has she been verbally abusive towards you, but she is showing a lack of respect for diversity. This may be an issue if she is allowed to remain in the centre. She should be removed from the premises.

Risk Assessment Exercise

In this exercise, you are a Probation Officer. You are currently dealing with a number of cases, all of varying severity. Study the short case descriptions below and then prioritise the case numbers from 1-4 (with 1 being the highest).

Make sure you include an explanation for why you have ordered your list in the way that you have. Keep hold of this list, because you'll be using it in the next exercise.

1. Marcus Clackson. Marcus is an older offender who has recently been paroled from prison, after receiving a 6 month sentence for violent behaviour. The incident occurred whilst he was watching football as his favourite bar, and now he must attend weekly anger management classes at his community centre. He is banned from the bar. Marcus is devastated by this verdict. You have tried to persuade him to attend live matches, but he claims only to enjoy watching from his comfy armchair in the bar.

Despite this, Marcus has shown a determination to find a job, and is attending regular interviews. He is currently living with his sister, but strongly desires independence. Marcus has an excellent probation attendance record, and seems to be on the road to recovery.

Unfortunately, there is an email in your inbox this morning informing you that Marcus did not attend his anger management session today. The message is from one of the community leaders, who is concerned about his no-show.

2. Ben Purst. Ben has been in prison for 7 weeks, and still has 6 years left to serve. He was taken into custody as a result of a physical altercation, in which he attacked his wife with a hammer, leaving her with severe injuries.

You have been working with Ben for approximately 9 weeks. As of yet, he is not responding well to life in prison. He complains that the other inmates are bullying him due to his accent. Ben is still in the process of fighting his sentence and believes that he has been imprisoned unfairly. He is yet to recognise his crime or mistakes, and is extremely argumentative when you try to negotiate with him.

This morning, you have an email in your inbox informing you that Ben has been racist towards others prisoners in the past week, and has been refusing to eat his meals. The email is from one of the prison officers, who is concerned that this could damage Ben's chances of release.

3. Max Brooks. Max is a recovering gambling addict, who has been on parole for 11 weeks now. He was imprisoned for stealing money from a shop till, in order to fund his habit. Max is currently flat sharing with a friend whom he knew before prison.

You have been meeting with Max two times a week for the past 3 months, both in and out of custody. As part of his parole conditions, Max must attend regular community meetings at least once a week, in order to curb his gambling habit.

When you get into work today, there is an email in your inbox informing you that Max's rent has not been paid for the past 2 months. You also have another email informing you that, after attending his community meeting, Max was seen visiting the local casino.

4. Lucas Hill. Lucas is nearing the end of a 5 year jail sentence. He was imprisoned for stealing funds from a charity. You have been assigned to prepare Lucas for life upon release, and to help integrate him back into the community.

Throughout his time in prison, Lucas has been a model inmate. He has worked in various sections of the jail, and has embraced religion. He spends long hours in the prison chapel, praying and consulting with the on-site pastor. In your recent meetings, Lucas has expressed excitement at his upcoming release. After numerous affairs, Lucas separated from his wife before prison, and is now keen to try dating. He has also shown an interest in setting up his own business.

Throughout his time in jail, Lucas has taken steps to educate himself. He is in the final stages of a legal degree, and was due to sit his penultimate exam on the previous day.

This morning there is an email in your inbox informing you that Lucas was removed from his exam, and disqualified, after the assessors caught him looking at notes written on a tissue.

How to answer this question:

When prioritising cases, you need to consider ALL of the facts and information at your disposal before coming to a decision. Technically, there is no right or wrong answer to the above exercise. What matters is that you can support your decisions with good logic and reasonable assumptions.

Below is an example of how you might have prioritised your list and the reasons why:

1. Ben Purst. In this situation, I would place Ben as my top priority. Not only is he damaging his health by refusing to eat, but his behaviour towards other inmates is completely unacceptable.

Discrimination should never be tolerated, and Ben is directly hurting his own chances of release by engaging in such activity.

The fact that Ben refuses to accept his own wrongdoing means that he has serious psychological issues to overcome. I would endeavour to see Ben as soon as possible, in order to come to a solution to this problem.

2. Max Brooks. I would place Max just behind Ben, as a high priority. The fact that he has been seen going into a casino, where he can engage in the very activity that led him to jail in the first place, is a major warning sign.

Furthermore, his unpaid rent is a matter of extreme importance. If Max ends up in financial debt, then it is probably fair to assume (based on his previous behaviour) that he will start taking major risks in order to pay it off. You need to see Max as soon as possible, to discuss what is going on. If necessary, interventional strategies may need to be enforced.

3. Lucas Hill. I would make Lucas my third priority. It is fair to assume that Lucas will be devastated by the outcome of his examination, and it is important to ascertain whether he was actively cheating or whether there had been a mistake.

There is likely to be an appeal or disciplinary meeting regarding the subject, and therefore it is your job to counsel Lucas beforehand.

4. Marcus Clackson. In this case, Marcus would be my final priority. While his skipping the meeting is a matter of concern, I would simply give him a call in order to ascertain why he did not attend, or arrange a sit down to discuss any concerns or issues that he is having.

Adaptability Exercise

Take a look at your list from the previous exercise. Let's say, for example, it reads:

1. Ben Purst
2. Max Brooks
3. Lucas Hill
4. Marcus Clackson

After reading through your emails, organising your timetable and prioritising your goals, you are ready to begin the day's work.

Then the circumstances change:

1. You receive an email informing you that Ben Purst has collapsed after refusing to eat for a week. He has been taken to a local hospital, where he is being treated in the intensive care ward. The medical team has described his condition as 'critical yet stable.'

2. You receive an email informing you that Max Brooks has in fact paid his half of the rent, it was his flatmate who hasn't paid. Furthermore, Max attended his community meeting and then went straight home. The casino witness was simply a case of mistaken identity.

3. You receive an email informing you that Lucas Hill has admitted to cheating in his examination. As a result, he has been disqualified from the degree, and will not receive his diploma.

4. You receive an email informing you that Marcus returned to the bar from which he is banned last night, and was involved in another physical altercation. While the police were not called, he has directly violated the terms of his parole and may now need to return to prison.

Using the above information, reprioritise your list, giving logical reasons as to why you have chosen that order.

How to answer this question:

Once again, there is no right or wrong answer to this exercise, as long as you have provided reasonable explanations for your decisions.

Below is an example of how you might have reprioritised your list:

1. Marcus Clackson. Marcus would now be my first priority, since he has directly violated the terms of his parole. You need to get to the bottom of what happened, and inform him of the consequences of his actions.

As his Probation Officer, and someone that has built a rapport with him, you can do this in a calm yet firm manner.

If Marcus does need to return to prison, then he will need someone to break the news in a professional manner.

2. Max Brooks. I would still keep Max as my second priority. This is because you need to find out why his flatmate isn't paying the bills, and emphasise that, regardless of who has paid their share, this will still impact both of them.

When keeping offenders on the straight and narrow, it's important that they mix with the right 'sort' of people. It might be the case that you encourage Max to move out of the flat, as his friend is clearly not a good influence.

3. Lucas Hill. Lucas would remain my third priority. While he has admitted to cheating, and been disqualified, the circumstances have not really changed.

You need to find out whether his cheating will affect his sentence, and then have a sit down to discuss the implications of his behaviour and how he is feeling about it.

4. Ben Purst. It might seem insensitive to move Ben to the bottom of the list, but the unfortunate reality is that there is nothing you can do for Ben at the present time.

Of course you should visit him to see how he is doing, but it is unlikely that you will actually be able to speak with him for a few days, and therefore you should deal with the other issues first.

If Ben does have any relatives or friends that you know of, you should endeavour to call them as soon as possible, to be notified if his situation changes.

Teamwork Exercise

In this exercise, you are a Probation Officer who has just been assigned a new offender. Ian has been sentenced to 6 years in prison, for his role in a series of burglaries committed by a larger gang of thieves.

He is not coping well with life in custody. Recent reports from his prison officer show concerns regarding the state of Ian's mental wellbeing.

The prison officer reports that Ian believes his 'powerful friends' will break him out of jail, and that he has demanded a games console in his cell. He is also refusing to eat. So far, none of his requests have been granted.

The staff at the prison are frustrated with Ian's failure to obey orders. They believe he has no discipline and no training to fall back on.

As his Probation Officer, it is your job to work with other individuals in the system to bring about a change in Ian's behaviour.

Using the table below, select the most effective, least effective and ineffective groups of service that you could include in this case:

	Most Effective	Least Effective	Ineffective
The services that you should include in this case are: the prison counselling team, the psychiatric team, the medical team, the disciplinary team, Ian's family.			
The services that you should include in this case are: the psychiatric team, the medical team, the pastoral team, other members of Ian's gang, the chief of police.			
The services that you should include in this case are: the prison counselling team, the medical team, and Ian's family.			

How to answer this question:

The most effective response would be to *"include the prison counselling team, psychiatric team, medical team, disciplinary team and Ian's family"*.

- This answer incorporates all of the main bodies that can make a real difference in this case. The counselling and psychiatric team can work with Ian to try and change his outlook on the situation; the medical team are essential since he is refusing to eat and his health needs to be monitored; the disciplinary team can provide an explanation as to what Ian can do to procure benefits whilst in custody, and finally Ian's family can provide emotional support.

The least effective response would be to *"include the psychiatric team, medical team, pastoral team, other members of Ian's gang and the chief of police"*.

- Not only does this miss out on crucial support groups, but it also includes irrelevant groups. Based on the information given, we have no idea whether Ian is religious or not, and it would be a terrible idea to have him make contact with other members of his gang. Finally, the chief of police is too high up to get involved in this case.

The ineffective response would be to *"include the counselling team, the medical team and Ian's family"*.

- This misses out crucial support groups, such as psychiatric and disciplinary support.

Role Play Report Exercise

In this exercise, you are a Probation Officer working with an offender who has been incarcerated for 3 months. The offender has 6 months left on his sentence. Recently, he has been breaking the rules of the prison by bullying new inmates, and swearing at other prisoners.

You have been working with the offender for a short period of time before his imprisonment, but it is only in the last few weeks that he has started having problems. It is your job to talk with him about his behaviour.

For the **initial stage** of this exercise, imagine that the offender has come in to meet with you. His name is Samuel Frost.

In the box below, write out how you would start off the meeting:

```



```

Sample response:

'Hi Sam, thank you for coming to see me today. I would like to talk to you about an issue that has been brought to my attention. It's been noticed that you've been bullying some of the new inmates and also swearing at other prisoners. What's been making you act in this manner?'

- At this point, the prisoner breaks down crying. He is clearly very upset about something. You need to demonstrate a caring and understanding nature.

In the box below, write out how you would respond to this:

```



```

Sample response:

'Hey, what's the problem? Tell me what's on your mind and how you're feeling? I fully understand that this is difficult for you, but you need to talk and get things off your chest.'

- The prisoner tells you that he has recently received a letter from his girlfriend at home, telling him that their relationship was over. He is angry about this, and therefore has started taking it out on the other inmates. Now you will have to demonstrate a firm, but empathetic attitude towards his issue.

In the box below, write out how you would respond to this:

Sample response:

'Oh no, that's terrible news, and I'm really sorry to hear that. I understand the anger that you must be feeling. However, as you can appreciate, your actions towards other prisoners aren't acceptable. It's at times like this that you need the support of other people, and you can only gain that support by treating people with respect. Can you understand that?'

- If the prisoner doesn't agree with you, then you need to demonstrate your resilience, by further explaining the situation. Once you have brought him round to your way of thinking, you can help him. This is where you can show your caring attitude, and your knowledge of how agencies such as counselling services could be of use. If you can persuade the offender to make use of these services, and agree on a plan of action, then this is even better.

In the box below, write out how you would respond to this:

Sample response:

'You are clearly going through a difficult time. I'm here to talk to you whenever you need it. Instead of shouting at other prisoners, how would you feel about getting involved in a counselling programme at the prison? This would allow you to talk through your issues in a private space, with someone who has experience of dealing with them. It's very important that you aren't carrying around negative emotions, as this will reflect badly on your behaviour and could damage your chances of release. I completely understand that you are feeling devastated by what has happened, and I will do everything that I can to help you through this difficult time.'

Once the prisoner has agreed to take part in the agreed programme, you can start to discuss the details of the programme and how often he will need to attend. This part of the discussion is known as 'clarification'. Here, you will go back over the details of the meeting, to confirm and reassure the individual that the issue is being dealt with. You should also make clear the implications of failing to meet the agreed targets.

Always remember that Probation Officers are there to provide support and guidance to offenders, and not to shout at them, punish them or judge them for their crimes.

In the next part of the exercise, you are to report on the details of the meeting to the prison officer in charge of handling the case. This should take the form of a short letter, outlining the main points. The prison officer is named Sergeant Rogers, and he is fairly new to the role. The two of you have only met once before.

One of the key things to remember about this exercise is that it demonstrates how you adapt your communicational methods to different types of people. As noted in the description of the case, you have known the offender for several months. Therefore, in your meeting, you do not need to be particularly formal. When addressing a report or proposal, you should write in a formal and concise manner, particularly if the letter is addressed to someone of a higher station than yourself.

<u>In the box below, write out your own sample letter, outlining the main facts of this meeting. (Try to keep your letter to 300 words or less).</u>

Sample response:

Dear Sergeant Rogers,

Please find below my notes regarding the meeting with Samuel Frost, case ID 278145.

In recent weeks, the offender has been swearing at and bullying other inmates. Repeated attempts to stop this behaviour have failed. As Samuel's Probation Officer, I sat down with him to discuss his behaviour. Further investigation revealed that Samuel is upset about the break-down of an outside relationship, and is therefore taking his anger out on those around him. After a lengthy discussion, in which I made clear the implications of continued bad behaviour, Samuel has agreed to enrol in a series of one-to-one counselling sessions held here at the prison.

I have already contacted the on-site counsellor, who has agreed to fit Samuel in at least once a week. Currently the scheduled time for this is at 2pm, every Wednesday. Between us we have agreed that Samuel should attend these sessions until the counsellor agrees that they are no longer necessary.

I have informed Samuel that a failure to attend these initial sessions will result in disciplinary action. He is free to contact me should he wish to discuss anything further, or attempt another solution.

I believe that this course of action is the best suited for both Samuel and for the safety of the other inmates. If you have any other concerns or suggestions, then please do not hesitate to contact me.

Yours sincerely,

_____

Hopefully the above exercise has given you a clearer indication of what probation work is all about. Remember that this example is just the tip of the iceberg; you are likely to experience difficult and stressful situations that far exceed the aforementioned.

As you progress through this guide, the situations we list will become more and more challenging to reflect the complex nature of Probation Officer work.

CHAPTER 3

Education and Experience

The first step in becoming a Probation Officer, is to apply for a role as a Probation Services Officer (PSO).

As a PSO, you will train on the job, specifically dealing with lower risk offenders. You will need to complete this training in order to become a fully qualified Probation Officer (PO).

The entry requirements for PSO are set considerably lower compared to roles as a fully experienced Probation Officer:

- A minimum of 4 GCSE's or any equivalent, particularly English.

- Substantial work experience within the field

- A Level 3 Diploma in probation practice. This will be completed during your first 12 months on the job, and is work based.

- A valid driving license.

- To be in good mental and physical condition, as the work is extremely tiring.

WORK EXPERIENCE

Before applying, it is highly recommended that you take a period of relevant work experience within the field. This is important for two reasons. Firstly, it is vital that you have a practical idea of what type of work you will be involved with as a Probation Officer.

While the notion of helping offenders and assisting in challenging situations might sound appealing, you cannot know whether you are someone who is able to handle this without first-hand experience.

Secondly, when submitting your application form, you are far more likely to be successful if you have shown an ability to deal with situations that are similar to those faced by Probation Officers.

It does not matter if your experience is voluntary or paid, as long as it is substantial and demonstrates that you have the capability to handle yourself in challenging situations. When it comes to the interview, you will need to answer competency based questions. This will require you to detail circumstances where your input was vital to solving the issue.

The more experience you have to draw upon, the better your responses will be.

There are a huge number of voluntary options available for aspiring Probation Officers:

Contact local youth centres and prisons

Whilst employed as a Probation Officer, you will spend large portions of your day-to-day life in these facilities. Therefore, volunteering to work for prison or youth centres is a fantastic way to increase your experience.

It will provide you with direct access to the type of individuals that you would be working with as a Probation Officer, or a Probation Services Officer, and help your application to stand out for employers.

You can find out more about youth groups in your area by using the following link: https://www.gov.uk/.

Contact your local probation service

What better way to gain experience, than by actually volunteering as an assistant to real Probation Officers? This will give you an amazing insight into the work that Probation Officers and Probation

Services Officers perform on a day-to-day basis. It will also look fantastic on your application form.

If you can demonstrate that you have actually worked with Probation Officers in the past, then you will come across far better to the assessors. This is particularly the case when answering interview questions. Answers that detail situations where you have actively aided officers with real probationary situations will be extremely valuable, and gain you huge bonus points with the assessors.

Contact local mental health services

Probation Officers are often required to deal with individuals who are not in a healthy state of mind. Offenders may be aggressive, depressed or withdrawn. They may not take kindly to your input.

First-hand experience in dealing with these type of issues will put you in strong position for the selection process.

You can find out details of your local mental health services via the following link: http://nhs.uk/service-search/.

Contact charities and homeless shelters.

Ultimately, working as a Probation Officer requires you to safeguard and protect individuals who are vulnerable and in need of help. While the people you help are still offenders, the large majority of them will simply be individuals who need assistance in getting their life back on track.

There will always be times when you need to be firm, and assert your authority, but overall a large part of your job role requires you to demonstrate a caring and empathetic attitude towards the people you work with.

Working in a homeless shelter or a charity of some sort, is a great way for you to demonstrate to employers that you can handle pressurised situations. It will put you in contact with vulnerable individuals who are in need of counselling, guidance and safeguarding. While most of them won't have committed a crime, working with them will allow you to put your skillset to the test, and gain invaluable experience.

EDUCATION

In order to be accepted for training as a Probation Services Officer, you will need to be a graduate with an honours degree in either:

- Criminology
- Police Studies
- Criminal Justice
- Behavioural Psychology

During your training as a Probation Services Officer, you will undertake a Level 4 Diploma in Community Justice (in the chapter 'Probation Services Officer' we have listed the types of modules that you can expect to take during your Diploma studies).

During your Probation Officer training, you will take further degrees and studies, which will enhance your abilities. All of the aforementioned degrees can be supported by relevant GCSE's and A Levels in subjects such as psychology, languages and citizenship.

If you are someone considering a career switch, then these options will also apply to you. Although the process will take longer, as you'll need relevant work experience and a degree, there is no reason that you can't make the switch.

If you have a previous career in law enforcement or as a prison officer, then you are in a fantastic position to succeed, and will already have a wealth of relevant work experience. Careers that will significantly enhance your chances of getting this job include working as a:

Prison Officer	Police Officer	Prison Warden	Social Worker	Counsel-lor	Psychol-ogist

CHAPTER 4

Probation Services Officer
Application Process

Once you have received your degree, you will need to start applying for jobs. The first place to look is online. Due to governmental changes (as of July 2014) up to 70% of Probation Services Officers and Probation Officers, are now employed by outside agencies, where previously they were employed by local probation trusts.

Below we have included a mock job description for a Probation Services Officer, to give you some idea of what you might expect to see:

PROBATION SERVICES OFFICER = JOB APPLICATION:

Our client has a vacancy for a Probation Services Officer to work in Ficshire. This vacancy has an initial 6 month contract and a pay rate of £19 per hour.

Duties include:

- Arranging, supervising and monitoring community work placements for offenders;

- Helping clients to gain relevant work or training;

- Helping clients with drug or alcohol rehabilitation;

- Assessing the risk that individuals might pose to the general public;

- Interviewing offenders in order to gather information.

Requirements:

To be eligible for this role, applicants will need at least one year of substantial experience in probation work or of working in a similar environment.

How to break down the application form:

When studying a job application, it is important to break down the key qualities that the application is looking for. This is best accomplished by breaking down the application form into manageable sections.

Below is a way in which the above application can be broken down in order to make it easier to understand:

'Arranging, supervising and monitoring community work placements for offenders'.

- This duty will require your ability to organise activities or placements for offenders.

- It will also require you to be an adaptable person, who is prepared to find alternative means to solve issues.

- Finally, you'll need to use risk assessment skills to establish whether the placement that you have arranged is suitable for the candidate who is taking it.

'Helping clients to gain relevant work or training'.

- This duty will require you to use your communicational skills, not only to persuade clients to carry out the work or training, but to establish how they are performing in the role.

- You'll have to use your teamwork skills, by meeting with the client's employer and discussing their progress, as well as your risk assessment skills. For example, if you have a client who was previously imprisoned for arson, you wouldn't get them a job working at a candle shop.

- Finally, you'll need to use your adaptability skills. If a client's work placement doesn't succeed, then you can't give up. You'll have to try something else.

'Helping clients with drug or alcohol rehabilitation'.

- Primarily, this duty will require you to use your communicational abilities. You will need to present yourself as a calm and understanding figure for clients who are distressed or struggling to cope with their addictions.

- You cannot physically stop these people from harming themselves, but you can act as a mentor figure and guide them in the right direction.

- This duty also requires your risk assessment skills, in establishing whether a client presents a threat to themselves or others, and whether they show respect for others.

- You'll need to be respectful and understanding at all times, and show a tolerance for other people's flaws and weaknesses.

- Finally, you'll need excellent team working skills, as you work in conjunction with addiction support professionals to provide the best possible service to both clients and the public.

'Interviewing offenders in order to gather information'.

- As a Probation Officer, your interview skills will be paramount to your ability to succeed in the role.

- In order to interview clients successfully, you'll need fantastic communication skills, as well as respect for others.

- This will also test your risk assessment skills. If you are taking large amounts of verbal abuse from a prisoner, then you will need to make a decision on how best to continue.

> 'Applicants will need at least one year of substantial experience in probation work or of working in a similar environment'.

- This application asks for a certain level of experience from candidates. This means that during the application form and interview stages, you will be expected to demonstrate how the skills you have learned and used in your previous job roles can be applied to the role.

- Your previous experience will therefore be absolutely key.

As you can see, although this is a relatively small/short job description, the core competencies that we outlined in the beginning of this guide will be absolutely crucial to your chances of success. Once you have applied for the job, the next stage will be to fill in an application form.

APPLICATION FORM

The Probation Services Officer application form will consist of a series of questions, assessing your background, previous employment and key skills. The form will generally look something like this:

FICSHIRE PROBATION SERVICES OFFICER APPLICATION FORM

Please complete all sections of this form in as much detail as possible. Your application form will be assessed against the personal specification given in the job description, and will be used to decide whether you will be selected for an interview.

Upon completion of this form, please send it directly to Ficshire HR department in advance of the closure date (October 3rd). All information will be entered into our recruitment database for monitory requirements, and will not be disclosed or shared with any third party, without your consent.

Personal Details

Position that you are applying for:

Job Reference Number:

Full Name:

Title:

Address:

Postcode:

National Insurance Number:

Email Address:

Home Telephone:

Mobile Telephone:

Are you in possession of a 2:1 (minimum) Bachelor's degree in any of the following (circle applicable): Criminology, Police Studies, Community Justice, Criminal Justice.

Education Details

In chronological order (starting with GCSE) please enter the details of your past, present or future education. This should include all schools, colleges and universities attended; GCSE's or equivalent, A Level's or equivalent, degrees and certificates.

Please be aware that you may be asked to provide documentation to support any qualifications listed during this section.

School/College/University: Details of Qualifications gained:

IT Skills

While you will not be required to have an advanced IT knowledge, we require all applicants to be knowledgeable to at least a basic level. Please circle the relevant response, to indicate which programmes you have used and are familiar with. You may be tested on the answers given in this section during the interview.

Microsoft Word:	Never Used/ Basic Knowledge/ Fully Competent / Expert
Microsoft Excel:	Never Used/ Basic Knowledge/ Fully Competent / Expert
Microsoft Power-Point:	Never Used/ Basic Knowledge/ Fully Competent / Expert
Email:	Never Used/ Basic Knowledge/ Fully Competent / Expert
National Delius:	Never Used/ Basic Knowledge/ Fully Competent / Expert

Experience

In 200 words or less, please summarise details of any past relevant experience that you have had, which is applicable to the role for which you are applying. This can include both paid and unpaid experience.

Please enter the details of any further training that you have received. Please note that you may be expected to provide evidence of this training.

Employment History

Please enter all of your employment history, starting with the most recent or present position that you have held.

Employers Name and Address:

Position Held:

Reason For Leaving:

Start Date-End Date:

Duties and Responsibilities:

Application Competency Questions

This is the most important part of the application form, and consequently is the area in which many candidates fall down. In this section, you'll be asked competency based questions that test your knowledge of the role and the core competencies required, as well as your motivations for joining the service.

Below we have listed several sample questions that you might encounter in this section, as well as sample responses to each.

In 200 words or less, explain how good organisation can impact upon the success or failure of a Probation Services Officer.

Sample response:

There are a number of reasons why organisation is important in this role. As Probation Services Officers, we are tasked with enormous amounts of responsibility. It's vital that officers are able to stay on top of things, so that they can provide a good service to clients. As Probation Services Officers, it is imperative that we can set a good example to both the public, and to the offenders we are working with. In order to perform the job successfully, we need to generate a level of faith and respect from all of the individuals we come into contact with. Keeping organised and on top of things is extremely important when it comes to submitting case files for review, general offender management and being called upon as a witness.

In 200 words or less, explain how an understanding of diversity is important for performing this job successfully.

Sample response:

Diversity is extremely important when working as a Probation Services Officer. Without an understanding and respect for diversity, it is not possible to treat everyone you meet in a fair and unbiased manner. Probation Services Officers need to have a good understanding of different cultural needs, and how as professionals we can adapt our service to meet those needs. Working for the probation service means providing a good service to everyone, and the best way to do this is to make sure that you have a comprehensive understanding of the needs of all members of society.

> **In 200 words or less, explain how an ability to work as part of a team is important for performing this job successfully.**

Sample response:

Teamwork is essential for Probation Services Officers. Officers need to be able to work with a wide variety of people, both inside and outside of the probation service. This includes working with: prison officers, voluntary agencies, police, legal teams, counsellors and psychiatrists, in order to provide the best service to the general public, and to the offenders. Rehabilitation is not a 'one man job'; it requires the dedicated input of many professional bodies. Probation Services Officers can ensure they are utilising all of the tools at their disposal, and perform their job to the absolute best of their ability.

> **In 200 words or less, explain why you want to work as a Probation Services Officer, and what has motivated you to apply.**

Sample response:

I have always been interested in the criminal justice system. My father was a police officer, and therefore I have been taught the values of the justice system from a very early age. I have grown up learning about the importance of offender management, and therefore it is only natural that I now am looking for a role within the sector. I believe that working as a Probation Services Officer would be a fantastic start to my career, and I have future ambitions to become a fully qualified Probation Officer. I'm a reliable, empathetic individual, with excellent communicational and team work abilities. I care deeply about safeguarding and protecting the general public, and I can think of no better way to do this than to join the probation service.

References

Following this, you will be asked to provide (at least 2) references, and finally you will need to complete an equal opportunities form.

Once your application form has been submitted, you will face a short wait before the organisation that you have applied to (whether it's National Offender Management Service 'NOMS', or an exterior service) considers your form.

The Next Step:

The next step after completing your application form is to undergo an NVQ whilst working as a Probation Services Officer. This is mandatory and will be required if you wish to further your career and become a qualified Probation Officer.

NVQ Level 4: Community Justice

The NVQ Level 4 qualification in Community Justice is essential to your career as an aspiring Probation Officer. You will have to work for at least a year in the post of Probation Services Officer, as well as completing an NVQ Level 4 in Community Justice.

The NVQ in Community Justice will teach you a number of key skills that you will need to be aware of if you wish to become a competent Probation Officer. The course will be taught using different modules, with each module focusing on a particular area of the Probation Officer's role. The NVQ will also teach legal framework, and further your understanding and abilities in the core competencies of the role.

We have outlined the typical modules that you should expect when studying for your NVQ:

Community Supervision

This unit focuses on the way in which Probation Officers carry out the fundamental supervisory aspects of their job, including planning, enforcing and monitoring community sentences. It deals specifically with the way that officers work with offenders who are not currently incarcerated, for one reason or another.

The topics in this unit will include:

- The impact that crime can have on victims and the way that Probation Officers can work to prevent this;

- How Probation Officers can conduct research into offender behaviour and then use it to influence and improve behavioural patterns;

- How Probation Officers can review and evaluate sentences, and produce interventional methods in accordance with these if necessary;

- The importance of clarification and ensuring that offenders fully understand their requirements during probation;

- Procedures for dealing with offenders who are considered 'high risk' or 'very high risk'

Equality and Diversity

This is a core module, which focuses on promoting equality and the value of diversity. As we have mentioned, a belief in equality and an understanding of diversity are fundamental qualities for any Probation Services Officer to have. All members of the justice department will need to be aware of, and be able to demonstrate these principles on a daily basis.

The topics in this unit will include:

- Legislation and employment policies;

- Equality and diversity codes of practice, and how they can be applied;

- Why equality and diversity are important and how they can be promoted;

- Discrimination, the different forms it can take, and the reasons for it;

- The effect that discrimination can have on individuals, communities and society;

- Why it is important for workers in the justice sector to understand equality and diversity;

- How cultural differences can affect the way in which different people interact with each other;

- How Probation Officers can behave in ways that support equality, challenge discrimination and show a respect for cultural differences;

- How Probation Officers can work with exterior agencies to promote diversity and equality.

Teamwork

This is a core unit that focuses on how individual officers can work as part of a team, and contribute to the quality of team efforts. The unit will teach the value of teamwork, how your actions can help the team to develop and how teamwork can be used when working as a Probation Officer.

The topics in this unit will include:

- Teamwork legislation, policies and procedures;

- How legislation, policy and procedural changes can affect your work;

- How to use your skills and competencies in the context of a team;

- How to demonstrate a respect for the skills and competencies of other members of your team;

- Why it is important to be efficient and utilise important resources when working as part of a team;

- How to help other team members improve their methods and how to recognise which methods are the most appropriate;

- Potential team based issues and how these could affect the quality of the work;

- How to address team based issues;

- How to use feedback to improve your team's performance and your individual performance as a member of the team.

Working with Exterior Parties

This unit focuses on the way in which Probation Officers can work with staff in other agencies, to deliver a good service. This is an essential skill for Probation Officers to have, and one that they will need to use on a daily basis. It is extremely important that work is fluently coordinated across all relevant agencies in the justice sector.

The topics in this unit will include:

- The legislation, policies and procedures that are relevant to working with exterior parties;

- A broad overview of the sector, including the details of which sectors are responsible for which tasks, how they function and the best way to communicate with them;

- How different working cultures and structures can impact joint-working;

- Potential issues with joint-working and why these might arise;

- How to prevent issues from happening and dealing with them if they do;

- How to identify which sector to contact and the ways that you would go about doing this.

Maintaining your Competencies

This unit focuses on individual development, and demonstrates key skills and competencies in line with company standards. It explores the relationship between employer and employee, the duty of care that employers have in aiding the development of their staff, and the duty that employees have in taking steps to better their performance and grow as professionals. This is a fundamental module for all members of the justice sector.

The topics in this unit will include:

- Why it is important for employees of the justice sector to maintain and improve their skills and competencies;

- How different people have different learning needs and speeds, and the importance of tailoring your attitude to suit the needs of everyone;

- The importance of appraisals and reviews, and how they can be used to better your performance;

- The importance of peer feedback in order to evaluate your own performance;

- Why it is important for employees to take responsibility for their own development;

- How employers can help employees to improve and better their performance.

Offender Behaviour

This unit focuses on the way in which probation workers can help offenders to understand and improve their behaviour. This is possibly the most important skill that a Probation Officer can have, so it is essential that you learn it. Officers need to have a full understanding of the factors that can lead to offending behaviour, and must be able to help individuals keep on the straight and narrow.

The topics in this unit will include:

- How psychological, social and emotional development can affect an individual's behavioural patterns;

- The impact that crime can have on victims;

- Different approaches and methods of helping offenders to see why their behaviour was wrong and encourage them to change this behaviour;

- Helping offenders to see the effect that their decisions have on others, and encourage them to take responsibility for their actions;

- The different communicational methods that can be used when working with different individuals and how to identify which approach to take;

- The importance of using equality, diversity and anti-discriminatory practices when working with offenders;

- How to identify when further expertise is required in dealing with offenders.

Probation Communication

This is a core module and focuses on the ways in which probation workers can communicate effectively with those they are dealing with. This includes offenders, exterior and internal agencies. You will be required to utilise both verbal and non-verbal forms of communication including emails, telephone calls and written recommendation forms. Good communication is absolutely essential for all members of the justice sector.

The topics in this unit will include:

• The legislation, policies and procedures that are relevant to communicating in the justice sector;

• The management, security and disclosure of information;

• How to improve communication, focusing on your weakest areas;

• The reasons why good communication is important in the justice sector workplace;

• Potential barriers to communication, including culture, gender, health, knowledge and language;

• The importance of clarification and allowing the person with whom you are communicating to ask questions;

• The importance of confidentiality and disclosing sensitive information only to people who have the right to, or need to, know it.

Health & Safety

As with any career, health and safety is absolutely essential in the justice sector. This is particularly the case when it comes to probation work, where officers are placed in extremely difficult situations. Probation Officers have a duty to take reasonable care in order to avoid any harm coming to themselves, the public or the offenders.

The topics in this unit will include:

- The legal health and safety duties of probation workers in the workplace;

- The legislation surrounding health and safety in the workplace;

- Workplace hazards and the importance of identifying them as early as possible;

- Taking responsibility for dealing with hazards in the workplace;

- Reporting health and safety matters to the relevant supervisors;

- Maintaining safe working practices in your job role.

Courts and Hearings

This unit deals specifically with the relationship between probation workers, courts and formal hearings. It is essential that probation workers have a good understanding of how the information that they provide in court and at hearings can be used, and what responsibilities and principles they need to adhere to when doing so. Probation Officers may be required to speak at, and submit evidence to criminal courts, civil courts, parole boards, mental health tribunals, childcare hearings, and appeal panels.

The topics in this unit will include:

- Statutory requirements and procedures;

- Hearing and court conclusions and the way that probation workers can affect these;

- The different forms of reports that are required for different forms of courts and hearings;

- The way in which probation workers need to adapt their communicational methods according to which agency they are working with.

- How to use the core competencies of respect for others and understanding diversity when providing evidence at hearings or in court.

Assessing Behaviour

This unit focuses on further offender management, assessing behaviour, developing change proposals and documenting reports in order to aid decisions. The unit will examine the fundamental skill of risk assessment, by using real life cases to demonstrate the way in which probation workers deal with their client. Primarily, the aim of the unit is to show Probation Officers how they can work to reduce offending behaviour, and safeguard the public.

The topics in this unit will include:

- The impact that crime can have on victims, and how probation workers can protect and respect the general public;

- The way in which research into known factors for offender behaviour can be used to reduce negative behavioural patterns and traits;

- How stereotyping and discrimination can negatively affect risk assessment, and how to prevent this;

- How to involve the individual themselves in the assessment, in order to produce a positive change in behaviour;

- The assessment reasoning process and how to come to logical conclusions;

- How to handle situations involving conflict.

As you can see, there are a huge variety of modules that you will take on your NVQ training course. The units we have listed are just some of many, all of which will introduce and help Probation Services Officers in terms of key concepts of probationary work.

Along with your module-based studies, you will spend the majority of your time in the actual probationary working environment. Probation Services Officers perform essentially the same work as Probation Officers, but work with much lower risk offenders. While this means the requirements for the role are much lower; the fundamental skillset is the same.

Your work experience as a Probation Services Officer will provide you with a basic framework to progress and succeed in the role of a Probation Officer, and therefore it is vital that you can draw upon this in your job application for the latter.

CHAPTER 5

*Probation Officer
Application Process*

Once you have completed a year's work as a Probation Services Officer, and completed the NVQ Level 4, you will be ready to move on and take the next step in becoming a fully qualified Probation Officer.

The process of becoming a Probation Officer is as follows:

- Initial Application Form;

- Assessment Centre, including written tests, presentations and psychometric tests;

- Probation Officer Interview;

- On the job training and further qualifications.

As you can see, the selection process is quite comprehensive. Over the next few chapters we'll take you through all of the stages, step-by-step, to give you an insight into how you can give yourself the best chance of becoming a Probation Officer.

PROBATION OFFICER = JOB APPLICATION:

Our client is looking for a qualified Probation or Probation Services Officer to work as part of a case management team, dealing directly with medium-high risk offenders. All applicants will need to have at least one year's experience working within the probationary sector, enforcing community orders and dealing with low-medium offenders.

Successful applicants will need to be responsible for their given caseload of low-high risk offenders, and must be able to perform the following duties:

- Rehabilitate offenders by enforcing conditions as laid out in their release license;

- Undertake risk assessment with the aim of protecting the public;

- Making offenders aware of the impact of their behaviour;

- Complete offender assessments using OASys and Delius;

- Maintain professional standards by undertaking regular assessments and reviews with the aim of delivering a constant high level of service.

Please fill in the attached application form, and send both that and a covering letter to the address listed on the top of the form.

How to break down the application form:

Just as we did before, let's break down this job description into manageable sections, and look at the core competencies that are required for each:

'Our client is looking for a qualified Probation or Probation Servicer Officer to work as part of a case management team, dealing directly with medium-high risk offenders'.

- The key words to pick out from this are *'case management'* and *'medium-high risk offenders'*.

- As we know, case management includes all of the core competencies that we mentioned earlier in this guide. It means that you'll need to have a firm grasp of all of the qualities that make for a successful Probation Officer.

- The fact that this job is advertising for someone to deal with medium-high risk offenders is also notable. It should give you a good idea of the type of people that you will be dealing with and whether you are equipped to handle this.

> *'Rehabilitate offenders by enforcing conditions as laid out in their release license'.*

- This means that applicants will need to demonstrate that they can be firm when required, in order to help with the rehabilitation of offenders.

- Part of being a good Probation Officer is knowing how to adapt your communicational methods to suit the situation that you are in, or the problem that you are faced with.

> *'Undertake risk assessment with the aim of protecting the public'.*

- As we know, risk assessment is a fundamental part of probation work. Probation Officers need to be able to perform risk assessment on a daily basis.

- They must be able to assess the risk that offenders pose to the public, and to themselves.

- This will be extremely important during the application form stage, and especially during the interviews.

> *'Making offenders aware of the impact of their behaviour'.*

- This falls under the core competency of communication.

- In order for rehabilitation to happen, it is essential that offenders are aware of the seriousness of their actions and can act responsibly to ensure that they don't reoffend.

- As a Probation Officer, it is your job to make them see this. You need to build a relationship with the offender to ensure that they respect you and your decisions.

'Complete offender assessments using OASys and Delius'.

- As we have mentioned, OASys is the probationary system that is used to perform risk assessment on offenders.

- Delius is the nationally used probation software. Thus, when working as a Probation Officer you will be expected to utilise both of these tools on a daily basis.

- Filling in OASys forms, entering information via Delius and using forms and software to track offender progress will take up large portions of your time. Thus, you need to be someone who is proficient in both areas.

'Send both that and a covering letter to the address listed at the top of the form'.

- Now, you will need to construct a covering letter. If you are not familiar with this, a covering letter usually precedes and is sent alongside a CV.

- It serves as a written introduction to your resume, and helps the employer get to know the candidate on a personal level.

- In your covering letter you should include your skills and interests, why you are applying for the role and your future ambitions. You should always tailor your covering letter to the role that you are applying for.

The Next Step:

While the probation system only uses online application forms for employees, some providers may still ask you to send in a cover letter so that they can get a more substantial overview of your skills and interests.

Write out a covering letter for the specification above, as if you were applying for the job role, and then compare it with the sample covering letter we have provided:

Sample response:

Dear Sir/Madam,

Please find attached my application for the position of Probation Officer. I believe that I would make an ideal candidate for this role. In the past year and a half I have worked as a Probation Services Officer for Ficshire Community Trust, as part of their offender management team. This involved working with low-medium risk offenders, in order to safeguard the local community and rehabilitate negative behavioural patterns. Whilst working as a Probation Services Officer, I completed an NVQ Level 4 in Community Justice, which equipped me with a fantastic range tools for working as a Probation Officer. My education has only complimented this. I took GCSE and A Level studies in behavioural psychology, foreign languages and citizenship, and I followed my psychology up to degree level. Alongside my work as a Probation Services Officer, I have a wealth of experience working in voluntary organisations across the country, including working at homeless shelters, mental health units and in youth centres. As a result, I have a fantastic grasp of the skills needed to work with vulnerable or challenging individuals. I'm now looking to move on to the next stage in my career, and I believe this would be a fantastic opportunity.

I would be extremely grateful if you could consider my application.

Yours sincerely

As you can see from the above sample covering letter, we have presented ourselves as someone who is extremely interested in working for the service, with a background that fully compliments the application by highlighting relevant education, skills and work experience.

Now, let's move onto the application itself. While the general layout of the application form will be extremely similar to that which we showed you in the application for Probation Services Officer, the competency questions are likely to be much more extensive, and will directly test you on the experience you picked up whilst working as a Probation Services Officer.

Below we've provided you with some of the competency questions you are most likely to see on the Probation Officer application form, and some useful tips on how to answer them.

Application Competency Questions

In 200 words or less, please give an example of a time when you have acted to combat discrimination.

Sample response:

When I was working for a voluntary agency, I was assigned to help a foreign homeless man choose clothes. Whilst out shopping at a local store, a gang of youths entered the shop. They began to hurl racial abuse and insults at the man, who was extremely distressed by this. I immediately acted and stood between the man and the youths, to try and protect him from any further abuse. I informed the youths that their behaviour would not be tolerated, and called the shop manager over. He asked the individuals to leave the shop, and informed me that the CCTV would have picked them up, allowing the police to deal with it. We then took the homeless man into the back of the store, made him a cup of tea and comforted him. I informed him that I would be more than willing to act as a witness for what I had just seen. Discrimination of any kind should not be tolerated.

In 200 words or less, please give an example of a time when you have used your communicational skills to resolve a difficult situation.

Sample response:

Whilst working as a Probation Services Officer, I was faced with a particularly challenging situation. The client that I had been assigned to deal with was somebody who had only recently been incarcerated, and was struggling to deal with life in custody. He was suffering from drug withdrawal symptoms, and this was only exasperated by his anger at being imprisoned (unfairly, in his view). It is fair to say that the first time I met with him, the client was on edge. I realised that part of the reason he was angry was because he felt that nobody was listening to him. To help him build trust in me, I sat and listened to him for over an hour, whilst he explained how he felt. I then used my skills of persuasion to suggest logical solutions to his problems. While this took at least 2 sessions, the client ultimately agreed with my suggestions and took them on board. Just by sitting and listening to him, I developed a great relationship and he ultimately developed into a model inmate.

In 200 words or less, please give an example of when you have used your risk assessment skills in the probationary environment.

Sample response:

Whilst working as a Probation Services Officer, I encountered a time when I had to make a particularly difficult decision on an inmate. The individual had been meeting with me for around 6 weeks. While these meetings had started positively, in the last few weeks the individual appeared despondent and extremely unhappy. He had a history of self-harm and suicide attempts, and therefore this behaviour put me on red alert. As a result of previous experiences, the offender had a fear of mental health institutions and would react with terror whenever the idea of being seen by a psychiatrist was raised. By our eighth meeting, the individual was barely speaking to me. He informed me that he was fed up with life. This forced me to make a risk assessment. If I contacted the psychiatric team, the prisoner might respond badly. If I did not, there was a threat to his life. Following the meeting I met with the chief prison officer, and we agreed that the individual should be given an emergency psychiatric assessment. I then contacted the psychiatrist who would be taking the assessment, to inform her of the situation. When the time came for the offender to be assessed, I personally informed him of what would take place, and tried to reassure him that we were acting for his safety and wellbeing. The offender reluctantly agreed to take part, and is now on the way to recovery.

In 200 words or less, please give an example of when you have worked as part of a team to solve a problem.

Sample response:

When working as a Probation Services Officer, I was part of a wider case management team tasked with rehabilitating offenders. My job was to correspond with the other officers in my team, and with other professionals, to provide a great service. On one occasion I was assigned a particularly difficult client. The individual in question had recently been released on probation, but was someone who had previous issues with drink, drugs and depression. As part of his probationary terms, he was required to take steps to help himself deal with these issues. I was tasked with locating relevant self-help groups, enrolling the individual and persuading him to go. Upon his attendance, I worked with the counsellors and group therapists to establish why the individual was behaving in the way that he did, in order to try and amend his behaviour. By using their professional advice, and applying my own knowledge of probationary skills, we were able to work together to successfully rehabilitate the offender;

ensuring that he did not violate the terms of his parole. Rehabilitation is a team effort, and cannot be achieved by one person alone.

In 200 words or less, please explain what has motivated you to apply for the role of Probation Officer.

Sample response:

I am someone who believes passionately in the value of offender management, and safeguarding the interests of the public. This has been taught to me from a very young age, as my father worked in law enforcement. My education and work experience mean that I am the perfect person for this role. A degree in behavioural psychology, combined with GCSE and A Levels in foreign languages and citizenship, will provide me with a fantastic platform upon which to utilise my skills. I have really enjoyed my time working as a Probation Services Officer, but now I believe it is time for me to move forward with my career. I would relish the challenges that this role has to bring, and believe I am extremely well equipped to deal with such issues. I think that I would make an enthusiastic, hard-working and experienced addition to your team.

CHAPTER 6

*Probation Officer
Assessment Centre*

If you are successful in your application form, you will be invited to attend an assessment centre at an undisclosed location. The assessment centre will require you to undertake a series of challenging exercises, both individually and as part of a team.

This will conclude with a final interview, whereby you will be tested on how well you fit the role personally, and assess your knowledge of the core competencies.

While the assessment tests can vary according to which provider you are applying to, the format is generally as follows:

- A written test;
- 1 or 2 presentations;
- Psychometric tests;
- A final interview.

Within this chapter, we'll go through each stage of the assessment centre, in hope to give you a better idea of what to expect.

We'll show you the type of questions you'll be asked and how to answer them, along with detailed explanations and tips for passing.

As with any assessment centre, the key is preparation and practice. Using our guide, you can ensure that you are 100% prepared for whatever questions you will face.

WRITTEN TEST

The written test is generally the first stage of the assessment centre. It lasts for up to 90 minutes, and is used to assess the following skills:

• Communication;

• Planning and Organising;

• Problem Solving;

• Adaptability and Flexibility.

Generally in the written test, you will be given an example scenario, and some basic information to go along with it. You'll have to read over all of this information and then produce a report documenting your decisions and the reasons that you have made them.

Written Test, Sample Exercise 1

You are part of a group who are responsible for the management of a large community centre based in a town called Fictown. The community centre has a large hall that can be divided into two different sections by using available partitioning screens.

Fictown has experienced many problems in recent times, particularly between different community groups. There has been much talk of racial tension amongst the different community groups. The local press has published many articles on the problems in the area and they are keen to promote any events that will diffuse the tension and problems. The community centre is fully booked every week. However, a slot has become available for four hours on a Tuesday evening and four different community groups have applied to use the centre during this period.

Your task is to decide which group(s) you are going to grant permission to use the centre on the Tuesday evening, 4th October 2015.

- You are to state the reasons why you have made your decision, including the reasons for rejecting specific groups, if this applies.

- You have been supplied with a recent press article and the application submissions from each group.

- You are advised to read the documentation carefully before creating your report based on the information available.

Recent article from Fictown Express

TROUBLE LIES AHEAD UNLESS SOMETHING IS DONE NOW!

As we are all acutely aware, there has been much tension in the town amongst local community groups. This has resulted in a number of arson attacks on local shops, and fighting is not uncommon on our streets. Whilst the Police are doing everything within their powers to calm the disorder, there is a growing concern that the problems are getting out of hand. It is time for action!

The Express has recently obtained news that the local community centre has received four applications from different community groups who want to use the vacant Tuesday evening slot. We understand that a number of the groups are unable to contribute financially and there are concerns that whoever the community centre management awards the slot to, there will be three other unhappy contenders. Basically, the centre management are in a lose-lose situation.

Further tensions and problems are likely to occur as a result of their decision. We are growing increasingly concerned for the problems in our community. During these difficult times we urge everybody to stay calm and try to work together in order to diffuse the tension in our town.

Applications

Group A:

A local group of predominantly white local residents who have lived in the area for many years. They have applied to use the centre on a Tuesday evening in order to display different films that will be open to the public. They are able to contribute significant financial funds in order to use the hall. They are also keen to show films that raise cultural awareness and understanding in the community.

Group B:

A small group of Polish residents who are new to the area. Only one member of the group speaks English and he is a competent translator. They want to use the centre on a Tuesday evening in order to talk about the problems they have encountered as new residents to the area. They will be inviting guest speakers to attend from the Local Race Equality Council in order to gain a better understanding of how they can obtain support whilst living in the community. They are unable to contribute financially in order to use the centre.

Group C:

A local school would like to use the centre on a Tuesday evening, to run educational workshops for 'problem' children. Some of the boys and girls at the school have been in trouble with the Police in recent times and the school would like to run the workshops in order to educate the boys and girls and get them back on track as law-abiding citizens. They are able to offer a small financial contribution.

Group D:

A group of Asian men and women would like to use the centre on the Tuesday evening to show films based around cultural awareness and diversity. The group are keen to raise cultural awareness in the community and want to do everything they can to work with different groups. Although they cannot financially contribute, they will be charging a small fee to people who view their films and this money will be given to a local charity or good cause.

How to answer this question:

The first thing you should do when looking at these questions is to draw out a list of pro's and con's. Take each group and look at the positives and negatives of each. For example:

Group A:

POSITIVES:	They are able to contribute significant financial funds; they are showing films which will raise cultural awareness and understanding; they have lived in the area for many years and therefore have respect from members of the community.
NEGATIVES:	N/A

Group B:

POSITIVES:	They are inviting guest speakers from the Local Race Equality Council; they are discussing race awareness problems.
NEGATIVES:	Their focus is only on the problems that they face as a group, and how they can get help, rather than aiding the wider community; they are unable to contribute financially to the centre.

Group C:

POSITIVES:	Educating young people; they can offer a small financial contribution.
NEGATIVES:	While young people misbehaving in the community is a concern, the news article and the task focuses on how we can fix racial awareness issues in the community, therefore it is not addressing the main issue; there is no indication that the arson attacks were committed by schoolchildren.

Group D:

POSITIVES:	The group are showing films based around cultural awareness and diversity; they want to encourage everyone to get along.
NEGATIVES:	They cannot financially contribute, but the fee charged will be given to a charity or good cause.

Using the above information, you now need to construct a report detailing your decision, and the reasons for it. Remember that this is a written test, so you should pay particular attention to:

- Spelling

- Punctuation

- Grammar

- Proper sentences

Write out your report in the space below, and then compare it with our sample response.

Sample response:

Dear Sir/Madam,

Please find detailed my recommendations and findings in relation to the issue of the community hall booking, on the 4th October 2015.

I have studied each of the applications and have come to the conclusion that the best suited applicant for the role would be *Group A*. The reason that I have decided upon this is that I believe *Group A* are in the best position to deliver a message that will help solve the problems that are plaguing our community. The group in question are showing cultural awareness films, with the aim of uniting the warring members of the community. While this is also the case for another of the applicants, the group have also shown that by doing this they will raise fairly significant funds for the community hall, which could be put to great use in solving other issues in the area. While the group in question are not made up of ethnic minorities, the majority of the members have lived in the area for several years and therefore have a healthy respect within the community.

In terms of the other applicants, there were 3 other candidates that I unfortunately recommend rejecting. While the community hall can be divided into two sections via partitioning screen, I believe that the noise problems resulting from this would inflict upon each party's presentation. Whilst *Group B* present a good case, they are fairly new to the area and their reasons for wanting to book the hall are predominantly for their own benefit. They wish to promote their own cause, rather than anyone else's. While this is perfectly acceptable, we should give priority to groups such as *A* or *D*, who are aiming to improve and aid the lives of everyone in the community, rather than just a select group. Furthermore, Group B only have one individual who can speak English, and cannot contribute financially for their use of the centre. *Group C* also present a compelling case, but their issues are not centred around the main issue. While it is admirable that they are looking to educate young people, and reduce crime, the main focus of the project is on solving the cultural awareness issues plaguing the community. Finally, while *Group D* would be my second choice, they cannot contribute financially to the cause. Instead, they have opted to charge a fee, which would generate proceeds for charity. While this is great, our focus should be on generating money for the community and local interests. Therefore, I would also recommend that they are rejected.

I hope that you find my recommendations to be useful, and that we can work together to produce a positive outcome for the wider community.

Yours sincerely,

_____

Now that you have seen an example of what the written test might look like, take a look at the following written exercises.

Written Test, Sample Exercise 2

You are the customer services officer for a fictitious retail centre. You have been asked to compile a report in relation to a number of complaints that have been made by shop owners, who state that rowdy youths are intimidating them at the centre. This is having a detrimental effect on their business. Visitor numbers at the centre are down 25% over the last 3 months.

CCTV reports suggest that a gang of 8 youths have been circling the centre during daylight shopping hours, often approaching customers and harassing them for spare change. The local newspaper have become aware of these incidents, and are sending a reporter to interview your manager. This interview will determine what the main problems are, and what the centre intends to do about them.

Your report should detail your main findings and also your recommendations as to ways to resolve the situation.

Use the following space to write up your main findings and suggest ways in which to resolve the situation.

Written Test, Sample Exercise 3

You are the customer services officer for a fictitious retail centre. Your manager has received a request from the Local Council Anti-Truancy Group, who wish to patrol the centre in groups of 6 people for a 5 day period next month.

During their request, the Anti-Truancy Group has raised concerns that school children from the local area are congregating at the retail centre during school hours. CCTV cameras have confirmed these reports. In a recent report, local police have confirmed that anti-social behaviour in the area of the retail centre has increased by 15% in the last four weeks alone.

You are to create a report for your manager that details your main findings and your recommendations.

Use the following space to write up your main findings and suggest ways in which to resolve the situation.

Written Test, Sample Exercise 4

You are the customer services officer for a fictitious retail centre. During a recent fire safety inspection at the centre, Local Fire Officers found a large number of fire escapes to be blocked with cardboard boxes that had been stored by shop owners. They also noticed that many of the areas were untidy and that the housekeeping was below an acceptable standard. Whilst the obstructions were removed, and the Fire Service will not be taking any further action, your manager is concerned that this type of incident will happen again.

He has asked you to create a report detailing your recommendations as to how this type of incident can be prevented in the future, and also how the standard of housekeeping can be improved.

Use the following space to write up your main findings and suggest ways in which to resolve the situation.

The Presentation

The next stage in the process is the presentation. This will be presented to and assessed by two examiners, and will last approximately ten minutes. In some cases, you might be asked to perform two presentations. The exact details and title of your presentation will be provided to you prior to attending, meaning that you will have ample time to prepare.

For many people, this stage is really difficult. They suffer from nerves and stage fright, out of fear of standing up in front of people and talking. The most effective way to get over this fear is to practice, preferably in front of as many people as you can. Ask your family and friends to sit down and listen to you present your topic to them, before you attend the assessment centre.

As with every element of the selection process, there are a number of criteria which you will be judged against during the presentation:

- Ability to relate to others;

- Communication;

- Planning and organising;

- Self-management;

- Problem-solving.

The title of the presentation will normally be based around one of the above qualities. For example, you might be asked to give a presentation on the steps that you took to solve a difficult problem. You will be assessed against the content and the way that you communicate the content to the assessors.

Once you have received your topic, you can start to plan links around it. For example, your presentation doesn't just have to be on the way that you solved a problem, it can focus on improvement for the future, the effectiveness of other solutions and how to maintain good service delivery. However, you should always try to keep your presentation relevant and on point, and ideally it should link to something you have achieved or done in probation work.

It is essential that the presentation is based around your OWN knowledge and experiences!

Now, let's take a look at the assessment areas individually, and look at how you can incorporate them into the presentation.

An Ability To Relate To Others:

This refers to the skill of being able to critically analyse relationships, and demonstrate self-awareness of the impact that your behaviour has on others. You need to be able to challenge inappropriate behaviour in a firm and diplomatic manner.

A great example of how you could use this in your presentation is:

'Whilst dealing with the problem, I was acutely aware of the impact that my actions would have on the other people I was working with. Therefore, I decided to ask them for feedback, in order to see how they felt about the situation'.

Communication:

Communication is a vital skill for any Probation Officer to have. You will need to have an ability to speak clearly, concisely and confidently, using language that is appropriate for the audience you are presenting to. This skill will be judged both as a separate topic, and over the course of your presentation as a whole.

Planning and Organising:

In order to be a successful Probation Officer, you will need to be someone who can plan and organise tasks in an efficient and effective manner. You must be able to prioritise effectively, and take a systematic approach to workload management, as well as being able to meet set deadlines. Furthermore, your planning and organising will be evident in how good your content is. If you have prepared in advance, then your content will be far superior than if you hadn't.

Self-Management:

This is extremely important as a Probation Officer. You need to keep yourself motivated, confident and aware of your own limitations, whilst still being able to identify realistic improvements that need to be made to your skillset. You must be able to use feedback to enhance your own performance, and take criticism constructively.

At the end of the presentation, you will be asked a number of questions that relate to this. These could include:

*   *How do you think you performed?*

*   *How did you prepare for this presentation?*

*   *Is there anything you think you could have done better?*

These questions are designed to see how you would analyse your own performance and whether you have the ability to identify areas for self-improvement. The assessors are looking to see whether you can take responsibility for your own development.

Problem Solving:

In order to demonstrate the key skills of problem solving, you'll need to show that you:

- Are logical in your approach to resolving issues;

- Can withstand substantial workload pressures, and examine every single option available before making decisions;

- Can take a flexible approach to resolving issues;

- Are an adaptable person who can change their problem solving methods when required;

- Can review your own progress when resolving issues.

How To Create A Presentation

So, how do you go about creating a suitable presentation? The answer is very simple, just take a logical approach. Whatever the title you are given, your approach towards it should be the same.

Let's look at a sample title, '**The Steps I Took To Solve A Specific Problem**':

The first thing you need to do is choose a suitable example to work from. This should be a factual, practical and relevant example, from your work or personal life. Think of times where you have had to solve a specific problem. The scenario you choose could be based on any of these, for example, it might be how you dealt with a difficult work colleague, or how you went about arranging a mortgage for yourself or your family. It does not matter what example you choose, as long as you are able to show the ability to handle that particular situation.

The second step is to break the presentation down into manageable sections. You should use the following process to do this:

Step 1: Introduction. Define the problem.

Step 2: Setting Goals. List what you hope to achieve.

Step 3: Alternative Solutions. Examining the other options available.

Step 4: Decision Making. Deciding how to solve the problem.

Step 5: Solution Implementation. Resolving the problem by taking action.

Step 6: Review. Analysing the above process, and understanding where you could have improved.

Now let's look at these steps in more detail:

Step 1: Introduction

During the introduction, you should introduce yourself to the assessors and then make sure they are comfortable before starting. Make sure that they can see the content clearly (via the project/PowerPoint/screen you are using) and then briefly explain the scenario. Describe the situation, who was involved and the problem you were faced with. This should last approximately 1 minute.

Step 2: Setting Goals

Now, explain what it was that you set out to achieve whilst solving the problem. A good example of this would be:

'After I had identified that there was a problem, I decided that my goal was to .....'

Step 3: Alternative Solutions

Next, explain what alternatives were available to you and the impact they might have. This demonstrates your ability to review a process, and consider all of the available options before making a decision. Make sure you explain the reasons why you didn't choose the alternative options.

Step 4: Decision Making

During this section of the presentation, you should explain how you reached your decision, and the reasons that you made that particular decision as opposed to others. For example:

'I then decided that the best course of action was... The reason I came to this conclusion was because....'

Step 5: Solution Implementation

During this stage of the presentation, you should explain what you did and what the result was based on the actions you took. Make sure that you make the result sound positive as a result of the decisions you made.

Step 6: Review

In the closing stages of your presentation, take the time to analyse what you did, and inform the assessors of what you would do differently next time. Then, explain that you are finished and wait to be invited to sit down.

Step 7: Final Questions

At the end of the presentation, every candidate will be asked a series of questions. These will generally include:

- *How do you think your presentation went?*

- *If you had the opportunity to do it again, would you do anything differently? Why?*

- *How did you prepare for this presentation?*

- *What do you think you could have done better?*

TOP TIPS FOR PRESENTATIONS

- Make sure you read the assessment criteria thoroughly, and then build your presentation around this.

- Give yourself plenty of time to prepare. Start to create your presentation title as soon as you receive it.

Helpful Tips

- Build your presentation in a logical and easy-to-read manner. Think about it from the assessors' point of view. How easy it is to mark? How well does it meet the criteria?

- Try to use keywords that relate to the assessment criteria. This will be a good trigger for the assessors when they are scoring your work.

- Practice makes perfect, especially in front of an audience. The more people, the better.

PSYCHOMETRIC TESTS

The third stage of the assessment centre is the psychometric tests. A psychometric test is based around the key skills and attributes that are required for the job role for which you are applying. The types of psychometric tests you will be expected to sit will very much depend on the position to which you are applying.

<u>The most common types of test you'll see during the probation officer selection process are:</u>

- **Numerical Reasoning.** This will test your mental arithmetic, data interpretation, quantitative reasoning, speed / distance / time, charts and graphs.

- **Non Verbal Reasoning.** Spatial, abstract and inductive reasoning.

- **Memory Tests.** Remember words or phrases over a set amount of time.

Although each type of psychometric test assesses different key skills and qualities, practising more than one type of psychometric test will guarantee to improve your chances of success.

If you know what kind of test you will be sitting, you can practice those types of question thoroughly. However, we suggest that you work through a number of different tests in order to better your chances. For example, you may be asked to complete a numerical reasoning test. It makes sense to practise mostly questions regarding numerical data, however, psychometric tests like concentration tests can also help to improve your speed and accuracy, and thus improve your overall performance.

Over the next few pages, we'll provide you with top tips and sample questions from each of these psychometric tests, to help you practice prior to your assessment.

How To Prepare For A Psychometric Test:

The only way to prepare for a psychometric test is to practice. Ultimately, the more you practice, the more likely you are to achieve higher marks, and thus better your chances of securing a job. It is crucial that when you get a practice question wrong, you take the time to find out why you got it wrong. Understanding the question is very important!

It is important that you find out as much information as possible about your test and what will be involved. There are many forms of psychometric testing, so you need to fully prepare for the test by understanding what is expected.

TOP TIPS FOR PSYCHOMETRIC TESTS:

- Before you sit your test, it is important to find out what type(s) of test you will be required to undertake. You should also take steps to find out if the tests will be timed, and also whether or not they will be 'multiple-choice' based questions.

Helpful Tips

- Even if you are only required to sit one type of test, we highly recommend that you attempt a variety of different testing questions. This will undoubtedly improve your overall ability.

- Confidence is an important part of the preparation stages. Have you ever sat a timed test and your mind goes blank? This is because your mind is focused on negative thoughts. If you practice plenty of test questions under timed conditions, then your confidence will grow.

- Do not spend too much time on one particular question. You may find some questions easier than others. You may struggle with a certain 'type' of question and so it is important not to ponder about questions you are unsure of. Move on, and then come back to those questions at the end.

- If you are unsure about the answers, make sure that you use our detailed answers and explanations to understand how to reach the correct answer. Knowing where you went wrong is just as important as getting the questions correct.

NUMERICAL REASONING

A Numerical Reasoning test is designed to assess mathematical knowledge through number-related assessments. These assessments will consist of different difficulty levels, and will all vary depending on who you are sitting the test for. Be sure to find out what type of Numerical Reasoning test you will be sitting, to ensure you make the most out of your preparation time.

TOP TIPS FOR NUMERICAL REASONING:

- Make sure you practice your mathematical skills. You will find the numerical reasoning test difficult if you are not great at maths. Practice your adding, subtracting, multiplying and dividing. You should also practice fractions, percentages and ratios.

- Try practising numerical test questions in your head, without writing down your workings out. This is very difficult to accomplish, but it is excellent practice for the real test. Also, try practicing numerical reasoning tests without a calculator. You do not want to rely on the use of a calculator.

• If you are permitted to use a calculator, make sure you know how to use one!

• Questions will often require you to identify what mathematical formulae is being used (division, percentage, ratio etc). Before you answer the question, carefully read what the question is asking you to do! Be sure to understand what you need to work out, before attempting to answer the question.

• Practice is key. The more you practice your mental arithmetic and other mathematical formulae; the easier it becomes. The more you practice these tests, the more likely you are to feel comfortable and confident with the questions. Remember, practice makes perfect!

• Make sure you pay attention to detail. Recognising units, measurements and other important mathematical formulas is crucial when it comes to your answer. If a question asks you to write your answer in centimetres, and you write your answer using millimetres, this is a careless mistake that is going to cost you easy marks!

Here are some of the most common numerical reasoning type questions, and how to go about solving them. We have also provided you with practice questions at a variety of difficulty levels to help you improve your numerical ability.

Adding Fractions

$$\frac{5}{7} + \frac{3}{5}$$

$$\frac{5}{7} \times \frac{3}{5} = \frac{25 + 21}{35} = \frac{46}{35} = 1\frac{11}{35}$$

Crossbow Method:

The CROSS looks like a multiplication sign and it tells you which numbers to multiply together.

One arm is saying 'multiply the 5 by the 5', and the other arm is saying 'multiply the 7 by the 3'.

The BOW says 'multiply the 2 numbers I am pointing at'. That is 7 times 5.

The answer is 35 and it goes **underneath** the line in the answer.

Subtracting Fractions

$$\frac{4}{7} - \frac{2}{5}$$

$$\frac{4}{7} \times \frac{2}{5} = \frac{20 - 14}{35} = \frac{6}{35}$$

To subtract fractions, the method is exactly the same. The only difference is, you minus the two numbers forming the top of the fraction, as opposed to adding them.

Multiplying Fractions

$$\frac{2}{3} \times \frac{4}{7}$$

$$\frac{2}{3} \times \frac{4}{7} = \frac{8}{21}$$

Arrow Method:

Multiplying fractions is easy. Draw two arrows through the two top numbers and the two bottom numbers (as shown above) and then multiply – simple!

Sometimes the fraction can be simplified, but in the above example, the answer is already in its simplest form.

Dividing Fractions

$$\frac{3}{7} \div \frac{1}{3}$$

$$\frac{3}{7} \div \frac{3}{1} = \frac{3}{7} \times \frac{3}{1} = \frac{9}{7} = 1\frac{2}{7}$$

Most people think that dividing fractions is difficult. However, it's actually relatively simple if you have mastered multiplying fractions.

Mathematicians realised that if you turn the second fraction upside down (like in the above example), and then change the 'divide' sum to a 'multiply', you will get the correct answer.

Fractions / Decimals / Percentages

$$\frac{1}{10} = 0.1 = 10\%$$

How to turn fractions into decimals, and decimals into percentages

- 0.1 into a percent, you would move the decimal point two places to the right, so it becomes 10%.

- To convert 1/10 into a decimal, you would divide both numbers. For example, $1 \div 10 = 0.1$.

- To convert 10% into a decimal, you move the decimal point two places to the left. For example, to convert 10% into a decimal, the decimal point moves two spaces to the left to become 0.1.

Simplifying Fractions

$$\frac{24}{30} = \frac{12}{15} = \frac{4}{5}$$

Simplifying Fractions

There are a few steps to follow in order to correctly simplify fractions.

- Can both numbers be divided by 2? If yes, then how many times does 2 go into each number? Write the new fraction.

- Using the new fraction, do the same thing. Can 2 go into both numbers? If yes, divide both numbers by 2.

- If both numbers cannot be divided by 2, then try the first odd number: 3. Can both numbers be divided by 3? If yes, divide both numbers by 3. Do this again until 3 no longer goes into the number.

- If 3 does not go into the numbers again, it doesn't mean it's finished. Try the next odd number: 5, and so on until the fraction can no longer be simplified.

Fractions and Numbers

What is $\frac{3}{7}$ of 700?

How to work it out:

- $700 \div 7 \times 3 = 300$.

Percentages

What is 45% of 500?

How to work it out

- To work out percentages, divide the whole number by 100 and then multiply the percentage you want to find.

- **For example:**
  - o $500 \div 100 \times 45 = 225$
  - o So, 225 is 45% of 500.

Volume

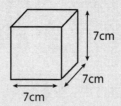

Volume

Length x base x height

- **7 x 7 x 7 = 343**

Areas / Perimeters

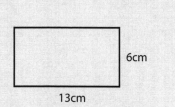

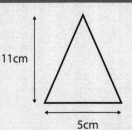

Area of squares / rectangles

Base x height

- $13 \times 6 = 78$ cm²

Area of triangles

½ base x height

- $11 \times 5 \div 2 = 27.5$

Perimeter

Add all the sizes of each side.

- $6 + 6 + 13 + 13 = 38$

Angles

Factors

Factors of 12:

Factors are all the numbers that can go into the number.

So, 1 × 12 = 12
2 × 6
3 × 4

So in ascending order, 1, 2, 3, 4, 6 and 12 are all factors of the number 12.

- Factors are numbers that can be divided into the number. For example; 6 has the factors of 1 and 6; 2 and 3.

Multiples

Multiples of 15

15	30	45	60	75	90
105	120	135	150	165	180

- A multiple is a number which is made from multiplying a number in the same pattern.

- For example, the multiples of 2 are: 2, 4, 6. 8, 10, 12, 14 etc.

Prime Numbers

2	3	5	7	11	13	17	19
23	29	31	37	41	43	47	53
59	61	67	71	73	79	83	89

A prime number is a number that can only be divided by 1 and itself.

• For example, no other numbers apart from 1 and 5 will go into 5.

Speed / Distance / Time

 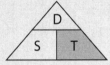 

To work out the Distance:

• Distance = Speed x Time

To work out the Time:

• Time = Distance ÷ Speed

To work out the Speed:

• Speed = Distance ÷ Time

Mean / Mode / Median/ Range

Mean

- To work out the mean of a set of data: you add up all the numbers and divide it by how many there are. (E.g. 4 + 4 + 6 + 6 + 5 = 25 - 5 = 5

Mode

- The mode is easily remembered by referring to it as the 'most'. What number occurs most throughout the data?

Median

- Once the data is in ascending order, you can then work out what number is the median. In other words, what number is in the middle? If no number is in the middle, use the two numbers that are both in the middle; add them up and divide by 2.

Range

- In ascending order, the range is from the smallest number to the biggest number.

Percent Increase

Work out the percentage increase.

Percent Increase

To work out the percentage increase of a set of data, you need to remember this formula:

Percent Increase % = Increase ÷ original number x 100

If your answer is a negative number, then this is a percentage **decrease.**

Percent Decrease

Work out the percentage decrease.

Percent Decrease

To work out the percentage decrease of a set of data, you need to remember this formula:

Percent Decrease % = Decrease ÷ original number x 100

If your answer is a negative number, then this is a percentage **increase.**

Now that you have a better understanding of the type of questions you are likely to face, have a go at the 30 practice questions we have provided. After you have completed the questions, use our detailed answers to see which ones you got correct, and which ones you got wrong.

Question 1

A charity arranges a bike race. 120 people take part. 1/3 of the people finish the race in under half an hour. How many people did not finish the race in under half an hour?

Answer

Question 2

What is 3/5 of 700?

Answer

Question 3

There is 4000 millilitres of water in jugs. If 1 litre is equivalent to 1000 millilitres, how many litres of water is there?

Answer

Question 4

What is the missing angle?

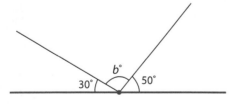

Answer

Question 5

What is 120 multiplied by 13?

Answer

Question 6

Find 60% of £45.

Answer

Question 7

How many lines of symmetry does this shape have?

Answer

Question 8

A packet of biscuits weighs 120 g. Find the weight of 9 packets of biscuits.

A	B	C	D
1080 kg	1880 g	1080 g	108 kg

Question 9

A squared field has a perimeter of 72 cm. What is the area of the squared field?

Answer [   ]

Question 10

What is 24/48 in its simplest form?

Answer [   ]

Study the following chart and answer questions 11-14.

Bike sales

Country	Jan	Feb	Mar	April	May	June	Total
UK	21	28	15	35	31	20	150
Germany	45	48	52	36	41	40	262
France	32	36	33	28	20	31	180
Brazil	42	41	37	32	35	28	215
Spain	22	26	17	30	24	22	141
Italy	33	35	38	28	29	38	201
Total	195	214	192	189	180	179	1149

Question 11

What percentage of the overall total was sold in April?

A	B	C	D	E
17.8%	17.2%	18.9%	16.4%	21.6%

Question 12

What percentage of the overall total sales were bikes' sold to the French importer? Rounded up to one decimal place.

A	B	C	D	E
15.7%	18.2%	18.9%	25.6%	24.5%

Question 13

What is the average number of units per month imported to Brazil over the first 4 months of the year?

A	B	C	D	E
28	24	32	38	40

Question 14

What month saw the biggest increase in total sales from the previous month?

A	B	C	D	E
January	February	March	April	May

Study the following chart and answer questions 15-18.

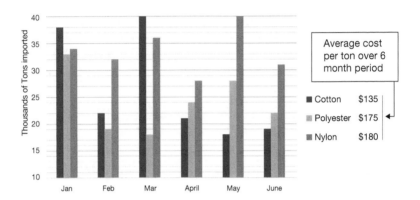

Question 15

What is the mean value for nylon imported over the 6 month period?

A	B	C	D	E
42.5	18.5	33.5	49.5	37.5

Question 16

What is the range for polyester imports across the 6 month period?

A	B	C	D	E
15	21	23	52	51

Question 17

What was the difference in thousands of tons between cotton material and nylon material imports in the first 3 months of the year?

A	B	C	D	E
5	15	24	17	2

Question 18

What was the approximate ratio of polyester and nylon material imports in the first 4 months of the year?

A	B	C	D	E
94:120	47:65	92:110	95:100	94:90

Question 19

There are 60 girls and 65 boys in the lunch hall at school. What is the ratio of girls to boys? Give your answer in its simplest form.

Answer

Question 20

Look carefully for the pattern, and then choose which pair of numbers comes next.

1,   3,   6,   10,   15,   21,   28

A	B	C	D	E
42, 56	42, 48	30, 36	32, 36	36, 45

Question 21

The set of data below shows the results in a year 11 Media mock exam. The marks are out of 100%. The teacher wants to find the mean mark for this test which was given to 68 pupils. Give your answer to 1 decimal place.

Media mock exam (%)	No. of pupils	No. of pupils X media mock exam (%)
10	0	10 x 0 = 0
20	2	20 x 2 = 40
30	3	
40	6	
50	8	
60	11	
70	8	
80	15	
90	12	
100	3	
Totals	68	

The mean mark is:

Question 22

The two way table shown compares pupils' results for GCSE English with GCSE Media grades.

English GCSE Grades	Media GCSE Grades								
	A*	A	B	C	D	E	F	U	Total
A*									
A		2	2	3					7
B		1	3	4				1	9
C			8	10	6	1			25
D				1		2			3
E								1	1
F									
U									
Total		3	13	18	6	3		2	45

The percentage of pupils who received a D grade in Media is approximately what? To the nearest whole number.

Answer

Question 23

A ruler is 30 cm in length, correct to the nearest centimetre. What is the smallest possible length of the ruler?

Answer

Question 24

The head of English created the following table showing the number of pupils in each year group who got a C grade or above in their test.

Year Group	No. of pupils	No. of pupils who achieved a C grade or above in their English test
7	86	56
8	93	48
9	102	72
10	99	52
11	106	85
12	68	56

What is the percentage of pupils in all the year groups combined that got a C grade or above in their test. Give your answer rounded to a whole number.

Answer

Question 25

Add 7/9 of 189 to 5/8 of 128.

Answer

Question 26

What is 9/11 of 88?

Answer

Question 27

An English class of 28 have just sat a mock Exam. The exam has 2 sections – Literature and Language. It takes approximately 6 minutes to mark the Literature section and 7 minutes to mark the Language section. Another 2 minutes is given on each exam to check the work again. How long in hours and minutes does it take to mark the English mock exam?

A	B	C	D
6 hours and 45 minutes	5 hours and 25 minutes	7 hours	9 hours and 10 minutes

Question 28

What is 0.9 as a percentage?

A	B	C	D
0.009%	0.9%	9%	90%

Question 29

Simplify x + 8x – 3x.

A	B	C	D
5x	6x	7x	12x

Question 30

Work out $23.7 - 2.5 \times 8$.

Answer

ANSWERS TO NUMERICAL REASONING

Q1. 80

EXPLANATION = 120 (total number of people) ÷ 3 = 40. This is equal to 1/3. Therefore: 40 x 2 = 80.

Q2. 420

EXPLANATION = 700 ÷ 5 x 3 = 420.

Q3. 4

EXPLANATION = there are 1000 millilitres in 1 litre, therefore if there is 4000 millilitres, that will be equivalent to 4 litres.

Q4. 100

EXPLANATION = the angle makes a straight line (which in essence, is a half turn of a circle). Therefore the angles would all need to add up to make 180°.   So, 180 – 50 – 30 = 100°.

Q5. 1560

EXPLANATION = 120 x 13 = 1560.

Q6. £27

EXPLANATION = £45 ÷ 100 x 60 = £27.

Q7. 0

EXPLANATION = this shape is a parallelogram, and these shapes do not contain a line of symmetry. No matter where you draw the reflection line, the shape cannot be reflected symmetrically.

Q8. C = 1080 g

EXPLANATION = 120 x 9 = 1080 g. Pay attention to the measurements; the question is in grams (g), so therefore your answer should also be in grams, unless stated otherwise.

Q9. 324 cm²

EXPLANATION = the key thing to remember is that the shape is a square (the sides will be the same length). If the perimeter of the shape is 72 cm. That means 72 needs to be divided by 4 (4 sides). So, 72 ÷ 4 = 18. Each side of the square is 18 cm, and to work out the area = 18 x 18 = 324 cm².

Q10. ½

EXPLANATION = 24/48, both numbers can be divide by 24. It goes into 24 once, and goes into 48 twice. Therefore it gives the fraction of ½.

Q11. D = 16.4

EXPLANATION = to work out the percentage overall total that was sold in April, divide how many bikes were sold in April (189) by the total (1149) and then multiply it by 100. (189 ÷ 1149 x 100 = 16.4).

Q12. A = 15.7%

EXPLANATION = to work out the overall percentage total that was sold to France, divide how many bikes were sold to France (180) by the total (1149) and then multiply it by 100. (180 ÷ 1149 x 100 = 15.66). Rounded up to 1 decimal place = 15.7.

Q13. D = 38

EXPLANATION = to work out the average number of units per month imported to Brazil over the first 4 months of the year, you add up the first 4 amounts (Jan-April) and then divide it by how many numbers there are (4). So, (42 + 41 + 37 + 32 = 152 ÷ 4 = 38).

Q14. B = February

EXPLANATION = to work out the biggest increase in total sales from the previous month, you work out the difference between the totals for each of the month and work out which has the biggest increase. Between January and February, there was an increase by 19. None of the other months have a bigger increase and therefore February is the correct answer.

Q15. C = 33.5

EXPLANATION = nylon material = 34 + 32 + 36 + 28 + 40 + 31 = 201 ÷ 6 = 33.5.

Q16. A = 15

EXPLANATION = to work out the range, find the smallest and highest number of polyester imports (18) and (33) So, 33 – 18 = 15 (thousands).

Q17. E = 2

EXPLANATION = to work out the difference, add up the first 3 months for cotton (38 + 22 + 40 = 100). Add up the first 3 months for nylon (34 + 32 + 36 = 102). So, the difference between cotton and nylon = 102 – 100 = 2 (thousands).

Q18. B = 47:65

EXPLANATION = 94,000:130,000. Divide both numbers by 2000 to give you 47:65.

Q19. 12 : 13

EXPLANATION = the ratio of girls to boys is 60:65. However, both sides of this ratio are divisible by 5. Dividing by 5 gives 12:13. 13 has no common factors (apart from 1). So the simplest form of the ratio is 12:13. This means there are 12 girls in the lunch hall for every 13 boys.

Q20. E = 36 and 45

EXPLANATION = this is a triangular number sequence. It uses the pattern of the number of dots which forms a triangle. By adding another row of dots (which increases by 1 each time) and counting all the dots, we can find the next number of the sequence.

Q21. 67.2%

EXPLANATION = add up the "number of pupils multiplied by media mock exam" and then divide it by the "number of pupils".

Media mock exam (%)	No. of pupils	No. of pupils X media mock exam (%)
10	0	10 x 0 = 0
20	2	20 x 2 = 40
30	3	30 x 3 =90
40	6	40 x 6 = 240
50	8	50 x 8 = 400
60	11	60 x 11 = 660
70	8	70 x 8 = 560
80	15	80 x 15 = 1200
90	12	90 x 12 = 1080
100	3	100 x 3 = 300
Totals		

So, 4570 ÷ 68 = 67.2%.

Q22. 13%

EXPLANATION = number of pupils who received a D grade in Media = 6.

Total number of pupils = 45.

So, 6 ÷ 45 x 100 = 13.333%. To the nearest whole number = 13%.

Q23. 29.5 cm

EXPLANATION = if 29.5 is rounded up to the nearest whole number, it becomes 30cm. If the number is less than 29.5, like 29.4, it would be rounded down to 29cm. Therefore, 29.5cm is the smallest possible length the ruler can be.

Q24. 67%

EXPLANATION = add up total number of pupils = 554.

Add up the number of pupils who achieved a C grade or above in English = 369.

To work out the overall percentage = 369 ÷ 554 x 100 = 66.6%.

To the nearest whole number = 67%.

Q25. 227

EXPLANATION = 189 ÷ 9 x 7 = 147.

128 ÷ 8 x 5 = 80.

So, 80 + 147 = 227.

Q26. 72

EXPLANATION = 88 ÷ 11 = 8 x 9 = 72.

Q27. C = 7 hours

EXPLANATION = total time spent marking one exam = 6 minutes (Literature) + 7 minutes (Language) + 2 minutes (checking) = 15 minutes. So, 28 exams will take = 15 (minutes) x 28 (exams) = 420 minutes. Converted into hours and minutes = 7 hours.

Q28. D = 90%

EXPLANATION = 0.9 x 100 = 90%.

Q29. B = 6x

EXPLANATION = x + 8x = 9x. So, 9x – 3x = 6x.

Q30. 169.6

EXPLANATION = 23.7 – 2.5 = 21.2 x 8 = 169.6.

NON VERBAL REASONING TESTS

Non-Verbal Reasoning tests are often used to assess a person's ability to recognise shapes and patterns in regards to formations. The questions appear in diagrammatic and pictorial form, and can be broken up into 3 categories: *Abstract, Spatial* or *Inductive Reasoning.*

The importance of Non-Verbal Reasoning tests is to determine how well you can understand and visualise information to solve problems. You need to be able to recognise and identify patterns amongst abstract shapes and images.

Non-Verbal Reasoning tests have become a popular tool for job selection processes, so it is imperative that you get to grips with each question type and know how to answer them.

Types of Non-Verbal Reasoning Questions

The type of questions that you will face in the Non-Verbal Reasoning test will vary depending on the type of test you will be sitting. This section provides you with a variety of sample questions and explanations, in order to give you a clearer understanding of what to expect.

Such tests may include:

- Determining identical shapes;

- Rotating shapes;

- Reflections of shapes;

- Finding the odd shape;

- Finding the missing shape;

- 3D shapes

Please note, Spatial Reasoning and Abstract Reasoning are very similar tests, but are different. Practising all types of questions can only work in your favour and better your chances of gaining a higher score.

Abstract (or Diagrammatic) – are tests to measure general intelligence. These tests require you to evaluate the rules surrounding the diagrams.

Spatial Reasoning – are tests which work with detailed and complex plans. Often, they rely on mental rotations of shapes through the use of coding, shading, colours, number sequences, data analysis etc.

TOP TIPS FOR NON-VERBAL REASONING

For many people, Non-Verbal Reasoning is extremely difficult. They are unfamiliar with the process, and unclear on where to start with answering.

Helpful Tips

The best way to begin, is with our top tips:

- Try and visualise the questions. This applies for all of the questions, especially the cube questions. This will help you to visualise where the shapes on the cube will be once you have folded the cube together.

- Non-Verbal Reasoning tests are designed to test people under strict time limits. Most people find it difficult to finish all of the questions. Therefore these tests are designed to measure people's level of accuracy whilst working in speedy conditions.

- Drawing or writing out your answers is a useful way to see what is going on. Drawing out the answers of what you think the shape will look like, will help you to visualise the answers.

- Using highlighters is a useful way of distinguishing your answers. Highlighting is helpful if you are counting lots of shapes or working out numbers of angles etc.

Below we have provided you with a list of the type of questions you should expect, and some tips on how to answer them:

Sequences

Work out which figure comes next in the sequence.

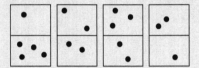

How to work it out

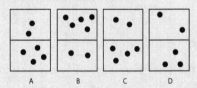

- The answer would be A. Starting from the first diagram in the top box, as it moves along the sequence it follows the pattern of 1, 2, 3, ... swapping from top to bottom box.

- Starting with the bottom part of the diagram, swapping from bottom to top box it follows the pattern 4, 2, 2, 2 ...

Answer

A

Odd One Out

Find the odd one out.

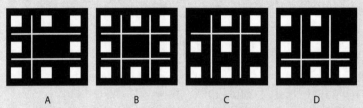

A B C D

How to work it out

- Pay attention to everything that is going on: colours, patterns, position, shapes etc.

- You should notice that figures A, C and D all contain three lines, whereas figure B contains 4 lines.

Complete the Series

Question

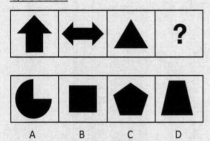

How to work it out

- Pay attention to symmetry, shades, shapes, size, patterns etc.

- You should notice that the first shape has one line of symmetry, the second has two, and the third has three.

- So you need a shape with four lines of symmetry to complete the series. Figure B (the square) has 4 lines of symmetry, therefore this would be the correct answer.

Answer

B

Rotations

Question

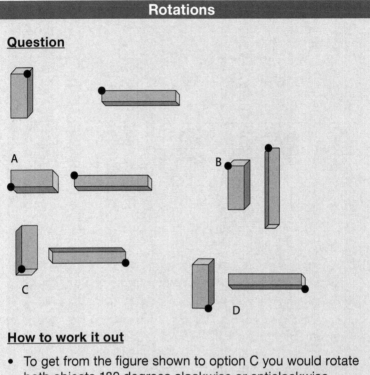

How to work it out

- To get from the figure shown to option C you would rotate both objects 180 degrees clockwise or anticlockwise.

- REMEMBER = both shapes need to be rotated exactly the same number of times, in the exact same direction.

Answer

C

Now that you've seen what the questions look like, have a go at the sample test below.

Question 1

Work out which figure is a top-down 2D view of the 3D shape.

3D Question figure

2D Views

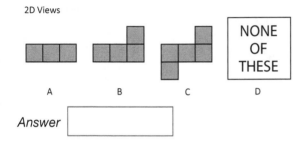

A   B   C   D

Answer

Question 2

Work out which option fits best in the missing square in order to complete the sequence.

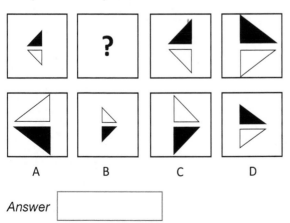

A   B   C   D

Answer

Question 3

Work out which 3D shapes from the answer figures are needed to create the Question Figure.

Question Figure

Answer Figures

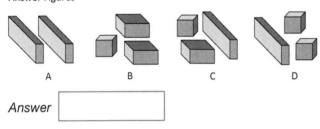

Answer

Question 4

Work out which 3D shapes from the answer figures are needed to create the Question Figure.

Question Figure

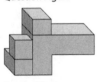

Answer Figures

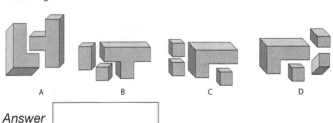

Answer

Question 5

Work out which of the cubes can be made from the net.

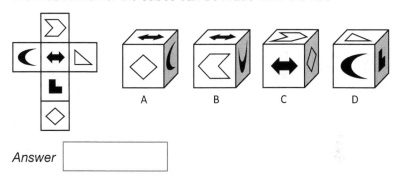

Answer

Question 6

Look at how the figure changes from box 1 to box 2. Apply the same changes in order to get the correct answer.

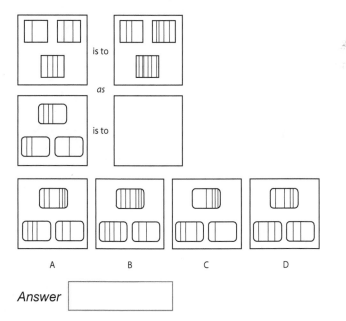

Answer

Question 7

Work out which option fits best in the missing square in order to complete the sequence.

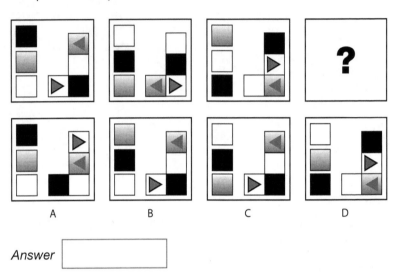

A   B   C   D

Answer

Question 8

Fill in the missing square in order to complete the grid.

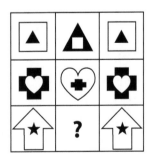

Answer

Question 9

Work out which option (A, B, C or D) would NOT look like the Question Figure if it was rotated.

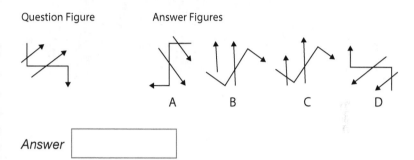

Answer

Question 10

Work out which option (A, B, C or D) would NOT look like the Question Figure if it was rotated.

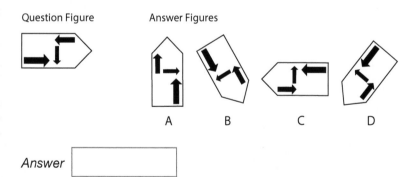

Answer

Question 11

Work out which figure (A, B, C or D) is the odd one out.

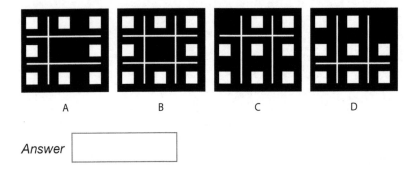

A   B   C   D

Answer

Question 12

Work out which option is a reflection of the Question Figure.

Question Figure

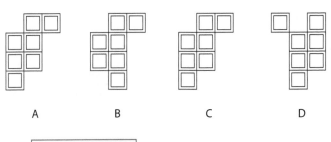

Answer Figures

A   B   C   D

Answer

Question 13

Work out which option (A, B, C or D) would NOT look like the Question Figure if it was rotated.

Question Figure   Answer Figures

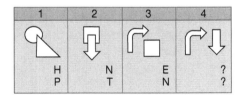

                          A   B   C   D

Answer

Question 14

Work out the codes for the figures and decide which answer has the correct code for Figure 4.

1	2	3	4
H P	N T	E N	? ?

A	B	C	D
P E	H T	N T	E T

Answer

Question 15

Work out which 3D shapes from the answer options are needed to create the Question Figure.

Question Figure

Answer Figures

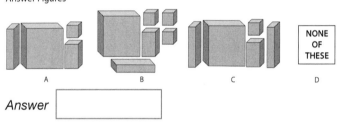

A   B   C   D

Answer

Question 16

Work out which figure is a top-down 2D view of the 3D Question Figure.

3D Question Figure

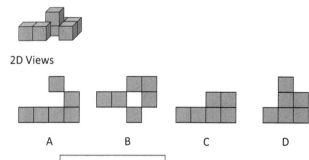

2D Views

A   B   C   D

Answer

Question 17

Work out the codes for the figures and decide which answer has the correct code for Figure 4.

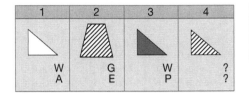

A	B	C	D
W	G	W	G
A	A	E	P

Answer [   ]

Question 18

Work out which option fits best in the missing square in order to complete the sequence.

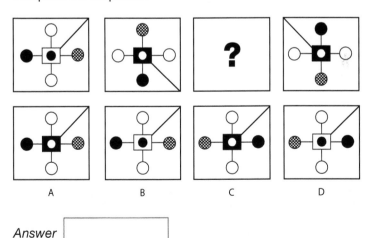

Answer [   ]

Question 19

Work out which of the cubes can be made from the net.

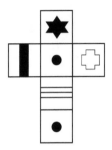

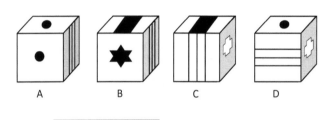

Answer

Question 20

Work out which two shapes are identical. (No rotation or reflection needed). TWO answers required.

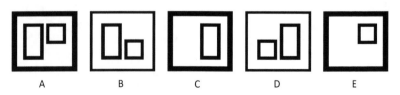

Answer

ANSWERS TO NON-VERBAL REASONING

Q1. A

EXPLANATION = a top-down view of the 3D Question Figure would show three squares in a horizontal line.

Q2. D

EXPLANATION = every even square has triangles pointing in the right direction, every odd square has triangles pointing in the left direction. The sequence progresses by the triangles getting bigger each time.

Q3.C

EXPLANATION = the Question Figure contains one cube, and two different sized cuboids.

Q4. D

EXPLANATION = the Question Figure contains an 'L' 3D shape, 2 cuboids the same length and a cube.

Q5. B

EXPLANATION = Figure A can be ruled out because above the diamond shape, there should be an 'L' shape. Figure C can be ruled out because the diamond and the two-sided arrow needs to be on opposite sides. Figure D can be ruled out because the triangle would need to be an arrow.

Q6. B

EXPLANATION = within the first set of shapes the corresponding lines within each square are doubling each time.

Q7. A

EXPLANATION = within each square of the series, the 3 squares to the left move down 1 as the sequence progresses. Within each square of the series, the 4 shapes to the right move up one as the sequence progresses.

Q8. C

EXPLANATION = the middle vertical box takes the shapes from the first row and swaps them around. For example, box 1 contains a triangle inside a square, which turns into a square inside a triangle. The colour pattern changes from white on the outside and black on the inside, to black on the outside and white on the inside and vice versa. Therefore the missing box needs to contain a white arrow inside a black star.

Q9. B

EXPLANATION = Figure B is the correct answer because the smaller arrow has been moved and is not touching the other line of the arrow. Therefore this is not an exact rotation of the Question Figure.

Q10. A

EXPLANATION = the arrow at the top of the Question Figure is in the incorrect position in Figure A. In Figure A, the arrow is pointing in the opposite direction.

Q11. B

EXPLANATION = Figure B is the odd one out because the other figures contain only three lines. Figure B contains four lines.

Q12. D

EXPLANATION = Figures A, B and C are all manipulations of the shape but are not reflections. Figure D is a reflection of the Question Figure.

Q13. A

EXPLANATION = Figure A is the correct answer because it is not identical to the Question Figure. The dotted squares should be diagonal to one another, however this figure places them side by side.

Q14. D

EXPLANATION = the circle appears once and is coded 'H'. A triangle appears once and is coded 'P'. An arrow pointing around to the right appears twice and is coded 'E'. A arrow pointing down appears twice and is coded 'T'. A square appears twice and is coded 'N'. Therefore Figure 4 needs the code of an arrow pointing to the right (which is 'E') and an arrow pointing downwards (which is 'T').

Q15. B

EXPLANATION = the Question Figure contains one large 'slim' cuboid, 3 cubes, and two cuboids (different size to one another).

Q16. C

EXPLANATION = a top-down view of the 3D Question Figure would show four squares in a horizontal line. It will have two squares above the last two squares.

Q17. C

EXPLANATION = a triangle appears three times and is coded 'W'. The triangles are two different colours. The white one is coded 'A' and the shaded one is coded 'P'. The four sided shape is coded 'G'. The stripes are coded 'E'. Therefore Figure 4 needs the code of a triangle (which is 'W') and for the striped colours (which is 'E').

Q18. B

EXPLANATION = within each square the diagonal line is moving round 90 degrees clockwise and the centred shape is moving 90 degrees anti-clockwise. You will also notice that the square and inner circle which form the centre of each shape are alternating between black and white.

Q19. D

EXPLANATION = Figure A can be ruled out because the two circles need to be on opposite sides. Figure B can be ruled out because the side with the three lines needs to be a circle instead. Figure C can be ruled out because the 'cross' sign would need to be a circle.

Q20. A and E

EXPLANATION = none of the other shapes are identical. Figures A and E are identical.

MEMORY TEST

The final stage in the psychometric testing process is the memory test. This is a fairly simple exercise, which will test your ability to remember large quantities of visual information in a short period of time.

During the memory test, you will be given a grid containing large numbers of words, similar to the example below:

account	noon	section	tube	corner	fruit
bear	folder	pottery	extract	thought	music
dew	office	point	store	wheel	life
brother	paper	rest	syrup	colour	belt
mind	thunder	hole	problem	magic	safe

You will be given 2 minutes to look at the grid, which will then be removed. Following this, you'll have another 2 minutes to remember as many words as possible, and write them down. You will be scored against how many words you can remember in the allotted time frame.

One fantastic way to prepare for these memory tests is to practice memory games such as **Pairs**. This is a card game in which all of the cards are laid face down on a surface. The aim of the game is to turn over matching pairs of cards.

You have 2 minutes in which to memorise the following words. Cover them up after the 2 minutes and write down as many words as you can remember in space provided.

Turtle	Problem	Flower	Money	Happiness	Sun
Landscape	Mine	Cloud	Boat	Jumper	Toothbrush
Egg	Spoon	Vase	Ant	Magnify	Kettle
Horse	Hot	Water	Soup	Leg	Alarm
Window	Rhubarb	Milk	Pastry	Curtain	Lifeguard

COVER THE WORDS!

What words can you remember?

You have 2 minutes in which to memorise the following words. Cover them up after the 2 minutes and write down as many words as you can remember in space provided.

Fence	Waterlily	House	Market	Orange	Goat
Marriage	Golf	Skip	Nightgown	Fishing	Temper
Foot	Data	Goose	Grid	Quest	Baby
Future	Allotment	Tax	Lightning	Gold	Hospital
Obstacle	Trousers	Exercise	Olympics	Ideal	Sample

COVER THE WORDS!

What words can you remember?

You have 2 minutes in which to memorise the following words. Cover them up after the 2 minutes and write down as many words as you can remember in space provided.

Lamp	Fork	Lizard	Star	Pony	Core
Interview	Success	Park	Public	Concentrate	Eyes
Critical	Beauty	Impression	Exhibit	Past	Book
Train	Shelf	Prepare	Danger	Clueless	Carpet
Pasta	Time	Yellow	Mango	Message	Bread

COVER THE WORDS!

What words can you remember?

You have 2 minutes in which to memorise the following words. Cover them up after the 2 minutes and write down as many words as you can remember in space provided.

Potential	Rabbit	Doubt	Fly	Under	Crisis
Kite	Bicycle	Glasses	Frog	Fire	Hide
Willow	Pocket	Beach	Rain	Slug	Garden
Blinds	Seek	Track	Date	Pet	Hammer
Lawnmower	Summer	Watch	Attempt	Pillow	Mother

COVER THE WORDS!

What words can you remember?

You have 2 minutes in which to memorise the following words. Cover them up after the 2 minutes and write down as many words as you can remember in space provided.

Doctor	Candle	Computer	Juice	Open	Rope
Sandwich	Bed	Energetic	Worm	Holiday	Plaster
Short	Fridge	Bingo	Scared	Film	Cake
Birthday	Hair	Grape	Large	Phone	Wax
Fragile	Words	Soil	Child	Pride	Tights

COVER THE WORDS!

What words can you remember?

You have 2 minutes in which to memorise the following words. Cover them up after the 2 minutes and write down as many words as you can remember in space provided.

Mission	Suit	Play	Sight	Different	Polite
Rage	Vision	Drive	Passion	Terminal	Pink
Pastel	Ignite	Ball	Lemon	Feather	Gherkin
Bird	Table	Queen	Opera	Paint	Snake
Balloon	Sardine	Coin	Cup	Quarter	Man

COVER THE WORDS!

What words can you remember?

You have 2 minutes in which to memorise the following words. Cover them up after the 2 minutes and write down as many words as you can remember in space provided.

Berry	Gamble	Show	Rainbow	Rattle	Happy
Pleasure	Satellite	Portrait	Leaves	Builder	Work
Hand	Seed	Speaker	Cry	Circle	Paper
Sky	Frantic	Cement	Stage	Blonde	Varnish
Field	Print	Pause	Autumn	Plane	Dumb

COVER THE WORDS!

What words can you remember?

You have 2 minutes in which to memorise the following words. Cover them up after the 2 minutes and write down as many words as you can remember in space provided.

Carnage	Rice	Flair	Elephant	Tea	Heights
Issue	Dance	Gap	Chicken	Revenge	Grandma
Shoes	Spider	Porridge	Wet	Fashion	Tear
Cold	Read	Teenager	Sweet	Clown	Drama
Castle	Papa	Coffee	Bitter	Punish	Noodle

COVER THE WORDS!

What words can you remember?

You have 2 minutes in which to memorise the following words. Cover them up after the 2 minutes and write down as many words as you can remember in space provided.

Chair	Shake	File	Fight	Pan	Gymnastics
Honey	Speed	Romance	User	Skate	Ponder
Sentence	Cheat	Ice	Officer	Mouse	Drastic
Battle	Pot	Jeopardy	Mist	Sweat	Horror
Mistake	Push	Police	Service	Distance	Suspect

COVER THE WORDS!

What words can you remember?

You have 2 minutes in which to memorise the following words. Cover them up after the 2 minutes and write down as many words as you can remember in space provided.

Electric	Shoulder	Strength	Examine	Staff	Carrot
Hamster	Fitness	Roast	Pyjamas	Tennis	Leopard
Rocket	Head	Plan	Jumbo	Oil	Hill
Chemical	Steam	Burger	Coconut	Physics	Spark
Swim	Propose	Direction	Cast	Lock	Racket

COVER THE WORDS!

What words can you remember?

CHAPTER 7

*Probation Officer
Interview*

If you are successful in your assessment centre, you will be invited to an interview. The speed at which this takes place will depend upon the provider to whom you are applying. For example, some providers might decide to have you take the interview at the actual assessment centre, whereas others may require you to wait and attend an interview at a separate location.

The interview itself will be conducted with 2 or 3 specialists within the field, usually with a Senior Probation Officer. In a sense, you can break your interview into two separate phases, *'the getting to know you phase'* and *'the competency phase'*. In the second phase, you'll be directly tested on how well you understand and can demonstrate the core competencies required for the role.

One mistake that many people make is to concentrate too much on the second phase, and ignore preparation for the first. This is a critical error. Remember that the first phase of the interview **sets the tone** for the second phase. If the interviewers get a terrible personal impression of you, then they simply won't be interested in how well you exhibit the core competencies.

Below we have listed a number of 'introductory questions' that you might be asked during the initial phase of the interview. To aid you in your preparation, we've given you in-depth sample answers to these questions. This will provide you with a template on which you can base your own answers:

Probation Officer Interview: Phase 1

Why do you want to become a Probation Officer?

This question requires you to demonstrate your knowledge of the role to the assessors. Probation work is extremely challenging, and therefore it's important for you to demonstrate that you are someone who is genuinely interested in the role, and that you care about making a difference.

You need to be as prepared as you can for any situation that you might face, as the consequences of going into this position unprepared could be fairly severe. For the assessors, the more knowledge you have about the role, the better. They do not want officers who will panic and give up early on in their career. Candidates who can demonstrate that they are aware of the difficulties that the job entails, but believe they can perform regardless, are far more likely to be successful.

In your answer, you should make specific reference to the impact that probation work has on the public, and on offenders, **in that order**. Always remember that as a Probation Officer, your primary duty of care is to the public. While you are entrusted with supervising and safeguarding offenders, you have a responsibility to work for the benefit of public safety at all times. If you can show the assessors that you are aware of this, you will greatly increase your chances of success.

Using the above information, write out your answer in the box provided, and then compare it with the sample response below.

Sample response:

I have always had a keen interest in the criminal justice system, and protecting the interests of the public. My late father was a police officer, and it is through him that I learned why it is important to manage offenders.

Whilst I was at school, I took GCSE modules in Psychology and English, and furthered both of these up at A Level, as well as taking modules in subjects such as Law and Sociology. As a result of these early studies, I gained a valuable insight into the justice system of this country, as well as methods of dealing with offenders. At university, I took an undergraduate degree in Community Justice. This equipped me with strong knowledge and practical experience within the field, as the course was both work and learning based. The work experience in particular was extremely valuable. In my second year, I spent a period of 3 months working alongside a Senior Probationary Officer in dealing with paroled offenders, to give me a better idea of what life within the sector is like. I learnt the value of teamwork, communication and responsibility from my probationary mentor, as well as invaluable behavioural analysis skills which I believe will aid me in the role. After I finished my undergraduate studies, I moved on to complete a Master's degree in Criminal Justice. This degree significantly furthered my expertise and equipped me with essential training in a number of key areas.

Following this, I used the skills that I had picked up during my degree in a variety of work experience placements. These include: working at a homeless shelter, performing voluntary work at a prison, assisting with young offenders at a detention centre and helping at a women's institute. Finally, I gained a position as a Probation Services Officer and completed a year of training, as well as working up to a Level 5 Diploma. As a result, I have worked with some of the most vulnerable members of society, and witnessed first-hand the effect that crime can have on members of the public. This has only strengthened my ambition to become a Probation Officer.

What are your key strengths?

This is a great question, as it allows you to highlight exactly why YOU should be hired. Your answer should essentially consist of all of the core competencies that we listed earlier in this guide. To recap, these are: *communication, respect for others, risk assessment, adaptability, team work* and *case management.* The best answers to this question will incorporate all of the key strengths into a clear and concise summary of why you are the best person for the position.

It is also extremely important because later on in the interview, during the competency based phase, you will be required to detail occasions when you have actively used these strengths to resolve a situation. Therefore, it's a great idea to 'introduce' these strengths to the interviewer.

Using the above information, write out your answer in the box provided, and then compare it with the sample response below.

Sample Response:

I have several key strengths, all of which make me an ideal candidate for this role. Firstly, I am a fantastic communicator and negotiator. I have developed this skill over a long period of time, and have extensive experience of negotiating and communicating with many different types of people. I understand that this job requires excellent communication with a number of parties, in particular offenders who might not necessarily be inclined to agree with all of my decisions.

Secondly, I have tremendous risk assessment skills. Throughout my training and my time as a PSO, I have demonstrated this on a number of occasions. I know that risk assessment is a vital part of the role, as Probation Officers need to be able to carefully balance out all of the pros and cons before making key decisions. Decision making is one of my strongest qualities, and I have no problem making difficult and unpopular decisions if necessary.

Thirdly, I'm an extremely adaptable person. I have shown an ability to adapt to difficult and challenging circumstances not just in my professional life, but throughout my personal life too. I have no doubt that I would be able to put this to good use whilst working as a Probation Officer.

Finally, I have excellent teamwork abilities. I have worked in a variety of different teams over the years, and I know that this experience will be extremely useful whilst working as a Probation Officer. I understand that Probation Officers need to work as part of a wider team of professionals; with the likes of the police, prison officers, voluntary agencies and even legal specialists, to ensure a good service to both the public and to the offenders under their priority.

What is your biggest weakness?

Be careful when answering this question. The worst answer that you can give here is, *'I have none'*. This will show a lack of self-awareness and humility to the interviewer. In a field such as probationary work, this could be a critical error.

You need to show that you are someone with the capacity for empathy, understanding and that you have a good understanding of behavioural psychology. On the other hand, you don't want to make yourself seem like a weak candidate. The best way to answer this question is to detail a weakness that could also be a strength. For example, you could tell the interviewer that your biggest weakness is that you sometimes struggle to delegate tasks, as you are a perfectionist and want to see every job done to the best of its ability.

Keep your answer short, succinct and to the point. You don't want to spend half the interview talking about your weaknesses as a candidate. Make sure you tell the interviewer in no uncertain terms that you have taken steps to improve your weakness, and believe this job could improve it.

Using the above information, write out your answer in the box provided, and then compare it with the sample response below.

Sample response:

My biggest weakness is that, at times, I struggle to delegate tasks. The reason for this is that I am a perfectionist, and want to see every task completed to the absolute best of its ability. This has led to problems in the past where individuals on my professional team complained that I was taking on too much work myself, and damaging the outcome of our task in the process.

After taking on board the feedback from my colleagues, I am pleased to say that I have worked hard at improving this. Although I am still determined to make sure every task is performed to its maximum, I am now more than happy to trust my colleagues with responsibilities that I previously only took myself.

I understand that it is vital to trust your fellow professionals with important responsibilities, and I am working hard to improve myself in this regard.

How well do you think that you deal with challenges?

This question is directly challenging both your knowledge of the role, and how you believe you would handle yourself in the position.

As you'll know from reading this book, working as a Probation Officer is an extremely challenging role, which will test you to your very limits. Every single day you will be faced with new obstacles to overcome, and on some days you might find yourself emotionally overwhelmed.

The interviewers need to know that you can handle all of this. They need to know that **you know** this is what you'll face, and that you want to do the job regardless of the difficulties.

As we have mentioned, the interviewers do not want to employ someone who will quit on the first day of the job. In your answer you should highlight that you are completely aware of how demanding the job can be, and that you are confident in your ability to overcome the challenges you will face.

Make sure you demonstrate that you are calm and composed under pressure, and have the ability to make logical and safe decisions regardless of the situation that you find yourself in. During the competency based phase of the interview, you will be tested extensively on your ability to deal with difficult scenarios.

Using the above information, write out your answer in the box provided, and then compare it with the sample response below.

Sample response:

I believe that I am someone who copes extremely well in challenging situations, and I take pride in my ability to think logically whilst under large amounts of pressure. I understand that this is a role where I will be mentally and emotionally tested on an hourly basis, and I am more than prepared to deal with this.

I believe that my previous work experience, and my time as a PSO, will greatly aid me in this endeavour. I have overcome multiple challenges in both my professional and personal life, many of which required tremendous emotional fortitude.

Whilst my time working as a PSO only involved working with lower risk offenders, I believe that the challenges it has presented me with will provide a fantastic platform for me to succeed in this role. It has given me crucial experience of working directly with offenders, and now I would love to take this experience to the next level.

What are you looking for from this position?

This is an interesting question, which should be fairly simple to answer. Here, the interviewer is looking for you to confirm that you are interested in this job for the right reasons. For example, if you were to answer, *'I'm just looking to make some money'*, then the interviewers could be fairly certain that you aren't the right person for the role.

A job as a Probation Officer is quite unlike any other position. You need to be absolutely dedicated and committed to role, and someone who genuinely cares about serving the best interests of the public by rehabilitating offenders. If you don't care about making a difference, or are unenthusiastic about the challenges ahead, then you are probably applying for the wrong job.

Just as before, the interviewers need to be sure that they are employing someone who is interested in the job for the long term, and not someone who will quit when the going gets tough.

Using the above information, write out your answer in the box provided, and then compare it with the sample response below.

Sample response:

I believe that this position satisfies everything that I am looking for in a job role. After completing my training as a PSO, I am ready to take the next steps into employment as a fully qualified Probation Officer.

I am someone who is looking for a job that can challenge me, with an emphasis upon helping the community. As a Probation Officer, my first duty would be to serve and safeguard the interests of the general public, and I can think of no better way to do this than by supervising and managing offenders.

Motivationally, I believe that this position is perfect for me. There is nothing that motivates me more than serving the best interests of the public, and the feeling of reward and satisfaction that I gained from my work as a PSO was absolutely invaluable.

Working as a Probation Officer would satisfy my need to help and improve the lives of others, and I am highly motivated to have the chance to do so.

COMPETENCY BASED QUESTIONS

The second phase of the interview will test your knowledge of the core competencies. You will be challenged on each and every single one of the competencies, so make sure that (prior to the interview), you have grasped the concept of each core competency.

<u>To recap, the core competencies for probation work are:</u>

- Communication

- Respect For Others

- Risk Assessment

- Adaptability

- Teamwork

- Case Management

During the competency based questions, you will be asked directly to give examples of when you have demonstrated these competencies in the past. For example, one question might ask you to give an example of when you have worked as part of a team to resolve a situation.

One fantastic technique for answering these types of questions is to use the STAR method. Below we have outlined the fundamental principles of this:

Situation

Start off your response to the question by explaining what the 'situation' was and who was involved.

Task

Once you have detailed the situation, explain what the 'task' was, or what needed to be done.

Action

Now explain what 'action' you took, and what action others took. Also explain why you took this particular course of action.

Result

Finally, explain what the outcome or result was following your actions. Try to demonstrate in your response that the result was positive because of the action that you took.

After working as a PSO, then you should have a plethora of examples to draw upon in order to show that you are the right person for the role. Voluntary examples are also a great way of demonstrating this.

The more ACTUAL offender based situations you can use, the better. While it is all well and good showing other examples of where you have demonstrated the competencies, the best candidates will be able to show that they already have experience of using these competencies in a probation based environment.

Over the next few pages, we have listed a number of competency based questions that you might expect to encounter in your interview, along with sample answers to each response.

> **Can you give me an example of when you have used your communicational ability to solve an issue?**

As we have mentioned, good communication is an essential element to probation work. At all times you will need to be a clear and effective communicator, who can relate to and calm difficult individuals. Your message needs to be crystal clear, whether you are sympathising with a struggling parolee or standing firm when it comes to an abusive inmate.

You need to establish yourself as the authority and use your communicational ability to relay this. Part of the challenge of being a Probation Officer is knowing which approach to take in certain situations. For instance, you could be firm with an inmate, thinking that this is the right approach to take, but when they react badly you might feel as if you took the wrong approach. Every situation is different and will test you in different ways.

A good answer to this question will not only display your communicational prowess, but will show that you approached the scenario in a logical and well thought out manner, and considered all of the variables before coming to any decisions.

Using the above information, write out your answer in the box provided, and then compare it with the sample response below.

Sample response:

Whilst training as a PSO, I spent large amounts of time working with young offenders. On one such occasion, I was dealing with a particularly difficult offender, who was aged 16 years old. The offender had recently been released from juvenile detention, but was already starting to show signs of relapsing back into bad behaviour. He had been caught drinking, smoking and was being abusive to his parents. As his Probation Officer, it was my job to manage this. I was determined not to let the individual sabotage himself.

Upon receiving a phone call from his mother, who was distressed about his behaviour, I immediately arranged a meeting with the offender. At first he was reluctant to do so, but I negotiated a time and place for us to meet. I then considered what approach I should take with the individual. In the past, I had been fairly lenient and sympathetic. This had clearly not had the desired impact. Therefore, I decided that it was time for me to show the individual, in no uncertain terms, that his behaviour would lead to him being placed back into custody.

On the day in question, I met with the boy at his home. After sitting down, I challenged him on his behaviour. Initially, he was unrepentant. He refused to accept any wrongdoing and would not listen to my suggestions. When pressed further, he grew angry. He demanded that I leave his home. Using my negotiation skills, I managed to calm him down and persuade him into discussing his behaviour with me. I calmly but firmly told him that while I was there to support him and help him improve, if he continued in this way then he would almost certainly be returning to custody. After a short discussion, the individual broke down in tears and confessed that he was ashamed of his actions. I sympathised with him but maintained my firm approach, as I believed this was the only way he would learn. The offender responded well to this approach, and together we agreed a plan of action, which included his participation in various support groups.

As a result of this meeting, the individual's behaviour improved significantly. He began attending regular support groups and mended his relationship with his parents. I am happy to say that there were no further incidents in the time that I was working with him, and he did not return to custody.

> **Can you give me an example of a time when you have demonstrated your ability to adapt to a difficult situation?**

Adaptability is a crucial element of probation work. Your daily life as a probation worker will require you to adapt to many difficult situations, and you will need to prioritise your decisions according to particular needs.

Earlier in the book we gave you a sample adaptability exercise that demonstrated how you will need to switch your thought process according to the needs of those that you are working with.

Remember that adaptability doesn't just apply to working with several different cases, there will many occasions when you will have to adapt the way you work in order to aid just one person. Every case will present you with different challenges and obstacles to overcome. You might go into a particular case with certain expectations, and then have them immediately subverted. You need to have the ability to deal with this, and respond accordingly. Flexibility is a fundamental part of the role.

Using the above information, write out your answer in the box provided, and then compare it with the sample response below.

Sample response:

I believe that I am an extremely adaptable person. One great example of this is the way that I have adapted to deal with probation work itself.

At the start of my PSO training, I am not ashamed to say that I struggled. I had undertaken work experience (alongside qualified Probation Officers) and volunteered in various sectors (assisting vulnerable people) but nothing prepared me for the difficulties that I faced in dealing with offenders on a one-to-one basis.

Many of the individuals that I was assigned to had no respect for me, and I was emotionally unequipped to deal with this. I knew that if I was going to succeed as a Probation Services Officer, and progress to the level of qualified Probation Officer, I needed to improve my performance.

The first thing I worked on was my approach to offenders. I am not a naturally firm person, and it was causing issues, as offenders were prone to taking advantage of me. Alongside my training, I enrolled myself in an exterior behavioural psychology course, and sought out the advice of qualified officers within the field. They provided me with invaluable advice on how to overcome my issues. I took this on board and immediately set about making changes to the way I work. I started taking a firmer approach to cases.

Upon exerting my authority, I found that the individuals I was working with responded much better. I found that I was able to adapt between this new firm approach and my previous sympathetic approach, according to the situation.

The more experience I got, the better this skill developed, and I now believe that I have adapted extremely well to deal with difficult situations.

> **Can you give me an example of a time when you have worked as part of a team to resolve an issue?**

As we have explained, teamwork is absolutely essentially for probation workers. While much of your time will be spent dealing with offenders on an individual basis, you will need to liaise with a wide variety of people in order to help solve issues. This means dealing with courts, prison officers, counsellors, voluntary agencies, relatives of offenders and medical staff, in order to provide the best possible service for offenders.

There are several key elements to working as a productive member of a team, not least communication. You'll need to be an excellent communicator and someone who is able to work with many different types of people in order to complete a task.

Working with outside agencies as a Probation Officer is particularly difficult, as many of these agencies will have their own agenda. You will need to negotiate on behalf of your client, whilst still remembering that your central duty is to protect the interests of the public. Rehabilitation is not something that can be done by one person alone, it takes the help and cooperation of multiple individuals working as part of a team.

Using the above information, write out your answer in the box provided, and then compare it with the sample response below.

Sample response:

Whilst working as a Probation Services Officer, I was placed in charge of a particularly difficult case. The girl, aged just 15, had a litany of mental health and personal issues, and problems with alcohol and drugs. She had experienced an extremely difficult up-bringing, suffering from abuse. The girl had reacted to this abuse with self-harm and unlawful behaviour.

I first began working with the individual just before she was released from custody. The girl was apprehensive about being released, believing that a return to the outside world would correspond with a return to drugs and alcohol. I was determined to make her see that this was a positive step, and that she could improve the quality of her life without returning to harmful substances. In order to do this, I felt that it would be useful to involve a number of other parties, both inside and outside the detention centre. My first step was to contact the on-site counsellor. The girl had had several appointments with this service, but little improvement had been made. I sat down and had a meeting with the counsellor in order to get a full overview of what he thought should be done.

Taking his advice on board, I got in touch with several exterior voluntary agencies to arrange support sessions for my client. Furthermore, knowing about my client's desire to one day work in the legal sector, I contacted an associate of mine and arranged for her to spend 2 days completing work experience by shadowing him. The individual was delighted when I informed her about this, and agreed that she would attend the support sessions I had arranged upon release.

Finally, I made contact with several members of her family, who had become estranged from the girl whilst she was in custody. I encouraged them to make contact with the girl, upon her release, and attempt a reconciliation. They agreed to do this.

From the point that she was released, the individual has been regularly attending both drug and alcohol awareness meetings, which have encouraged her to open up about the way she is feeling. She had a fantastic experience at the legal firm and is now pursuing the idea of studying a legal degree. Although the initial reconciliation with her family did not go as planned, I am pleased to say that the family relationship has now significantly improved and the girl has a much stronger support structure in place.

With the help of myself, her family and voluntary services, the girl has pieced her life back together and is now on her way to becoming an upstanding member of the community.

Can you give me an example of a time when you have acted to combat discrimination?

This question requires you to demonstrate your respect for diversity and for others. This is extremely important when working as a Probation Officer, where you will need to treat every single person that you meet in a fair and unbiased manner.

It is imperative that you have a good understanding and respect for all people, of different cultures and backgrounds, and that you can demonstrate that you are someone who will not tolerate discrimination of any kind.

Using the above information, write out your answer in the box provided, and then compare it with the sample response below.

Sample response:

Whilst working for a voluntary agency, I was assigned to assist an elderly, ethnic homeless woman in selecting some new clothes. Whilst I was helping her, a gang of teenagers entered the shop. They started to make racist comments towards the woman. I was disgusted by this, and extremely concerned for the individual to whom they were addressing their remarks. I was determined to put a stop to it, and protect the woman.

The first thing that I did was to stand between the woman and the racist individuals, to shield her from any further comments or abuse. I told the individuals that their comments were not acceptable, and that they were in conflict with the law.

I then called over the shop manager for assistance. He immediately rang the police, and asked the teenagers to leave the store. He informed me that the shop CCTV cameras would have recorded the offending individuals, and therefore the police would be able to handle the issue from there. After the individuals had left, the manager took me and the elderly lady in the back of the shop, sat us down and made the woman a coffee. I comforted her and informed her that I would be happy to act as a witness for what I had just seen.

The end result of this was that the individuals in question were prosecuted in court, and the woman did not suffer any further abuse. I believe that my actions were imperative in comforting, supporting and making her feel as if she was protected from their racist behaviour.

Discrimination of any kind should not be tolerated, and I will always take a stand against such behaviour.

Can you give me an example of a time when you have used risk assessment skills to make a difficult decision?

As we have explained, risk assessment and decision making is a fundamental element of working as a Probation Officer. You will need to make difficult decisions on a daily basis. The best way to arrive at logical decisions, is to use risk assessment skills.

You'll need to show that you have given consideration for both the safety of the offender and, more importantly, for the safety of the public. Remember that, no matter how close you are to an offender, your primary duty of care is for the safety of civilians. If you feel that the offender's behaviour is in contrast to this, you will need to act accordingly.

Good decision making involves balancing out all of the pros and cons, in order to arrive at unbiased and safe conclusions. Your decision making will be tested to its maximum potential when working as a Probation Officer, so it's extremely important that you can demonstrate your risk assessment skills in the interview.

Remember to use the OASys guidelines, as we outlined in Chapter 1 of this guide.

Using the above information, write out your answer in the box provided, and then compare it with the sample response below.

Sample response:

When working as a Probation Services Officer, I was required to utilise my risk assessment and decision making skills on a regular basis. On one such occasion that I can remember, I was assigned to work with a teenage boy who was being considered for release. I had been working with this individual for several weeks, to prepare him for his expected parole, and we had built up a close relationship. Unfortunately, the boy had started severely misbehaving. He had been bullying other inmates at the detention centre, answering back to officers and fighting with colleagues. He had also been caught stealing from the canteen area.

I arranged a meeting with the individual in question, to discuss why he was behaving in this way. I initially took an empathetic and supportive approach, in order to ascertain whether there were any personal reasons for his actions. Unfortunately, the individual was extremely unrepentant. He was rude and refused my request for help, claiming that his behaviour was justified. When I informed him that his actions were damaging his chances of release, he told me that he did not care. The boy refused to cooperate, and left with the issues unresolved.

The following day, I was due to act as a referral at the individual's parole hearing. As someone who had built up a good relationship with the boy, my judgement was considered key to the case. If I gave the individual a good referral, he was more likely to be released. I had to balance out the pros and cons. I considered the safety of the public against the boy's recent and past behaviour. While his past behaviour had been good enough to bring forward his release date, his recent behaviour was completely contrary to this, and suggested that he had not learned from the experience. If the boy was released, given his recent actions, we would be sending the message that his behaviour was okay. I felt that he clearly needed to spend more time in custody, to realise the seriousness of his actions, and that is why I recommended to the parole board that his release date be moved back.

While this was not an easy decision to make, I believed that the boy presented a risk to the general public. His recent actions suggested that he was not yet fully rehabilitated, and therefore it would not have been acceptable to recommend him for parole. The end result of this was that the individual was detained in custody for several more months, but left as a responsible citizen, who presented less of a risk to the general public. I believe my actions were fundamental in allowing this to happen.

Do you have any questions for me?

Once you hear this question, you will have reached the final stage of the interview. The big mistake that many candidates make at this stage, is that they switch off. They assume the interview is finished, and give a half-hearted response, such as 'No, I think you've told me everything I need to know'. This is an enormous error of judgement.

A failure to ask questions shows a lack of interest in the organisation, their goals and the job role for which you are applying. It will make you seem unenthusiastic. When it comes to probationary work, you will need endless amounts of enthusiasm in order to combat the difficult situations that you'll face. Thus, a failure to ask questions could severely damage your chances of getting the role.

The interviewers want you to show that you are interested in, and passionate about the job. Before your interview, write out a list of at least 6 questions that you want to ask at the end of the interview. This way, even if one or two of your questions are covered during the interview, you'll still have others to ask. Make sure that you listen carefully to what the interviewers have to say, and be ready to ask more questions off the back of their responses.

Here are a list of questions that you could ask at the end of your Probation Officer interview:

- *What on the job training will I receive?*

- *How many cases will I be assigned on an initial basis?*

- *What opportunities for progression are there?*

- *Do you have any reservations about my ability to do the job?*

- *What are the future goals of the organisation?*

- *Against what categories will my performance as a Probation Officer be judged?*

CHAPTER 8

*A Day In The Life Of
A Probation Officer*

Now that you are officially employed as a Probation Officer, you can begin working on individual cases. In this chapter, we'll run through the daily lives of two Probation Officers, to give you some idea of what life in the field is really like. We'll show you how they manage their time, how they prioritise cases and how they cope with the challenges their job entails. Probation work is mentally taxing, and you will need to be fully prepared prior to pursuing a career in the field.

Without further ado, let's meet our 2 Probation Officers:

- **Mark.** Mark is 45 years old, and has been working as a Probation Officer for 12 years. He manages a high case-load of both male and female offenders.

- **Gemma.** Gemma is 32 years old, and has been working as a Probation Officer for 2 years. She deals primarily with male offenders.

MARK'S DAY

7am:

Mark's day begins at 7am. After getting up and dropping his kids off at school, he makes his way to his local office base. Once there, Mark checks through his appointment book for the day, and looks through his emails. As he explains, this is extremely important:

'Sometimes I have urgent emails from the night before that change my outlook on the day. I spend at least 1 hour, 2 mornings a week, rearranging my priorities according to how things have developed overnight.'

On this occasion, Mark changes two appointments around to accommodate overnight developments. After making calls to inform the appropriate people of his changes, he begins his first task of the day.

8am:

Mark's first task is to write a letter of recommendation. This is for a client who has recently finished a short term sentence in jail, and is now looking to gain their driving license back. The client in question has just completed a drink driving awareness programme. Mark is cautious about writing this recommendation letter, as he knows that the client has a history of issues with alcohol, but recent behaviour suggests that the individual has reached a turning point. Mark advises that the client should be given his license back, but that strict sanctions should be enforced should the individual break the law again. As Mark explains, it's tough remaining impartial:

'It's hard when you've built up a relationship with someone. You want them to get better, but ultimately my job is to work for the best interests of public safety. If I think that person poses a risk to the public, then I have to act on that. If I write a recommendation letter, and as a result someone gets killed because my client was out drink driving, then I'm largely responsible.'

9am:

The next task for Mark is to deal with an email that he received the night before. Originally, Mark was scheduled to see his first client later on during that day, yet he opens an email to find that Bob relapsed last night. Bob claims to have lost £600 playing Roulette online. He was jailed for stealing to fund his habit, for approximately 8 months. He has recently been paroled from prison.

Due to Bob relapsing, Mark now has to prioritise his appointment with Bob as urgent, and decides to meet up with him this morning. Mark meets with Bob at his home, just ten minutes away, and sits down for an hour long consultation. Bob has been attending gambling awareness sessions twice a week, for the past three weeks now. The aim of the consultation is for Mark to establish whether the sessions are improving his behaviour, his risk of future crimes and to form future plans for improvement.

During the meeting, Mark tries to establish exactly what it was that made Bob relapse in the way that he did. This is important, because in order for him to help Bob, he needs to work out trigger factors for Bob's issue. So far, Bob has only been attending weekly gambling awareness meetings. Mark decides that the problem needs to be tackled in a more direct manner, and persuades Bob to begin a course in behavioural therapy at his local priory. He personally rings the priory to schedule an appointment for 2 days' time, and agrees to take Bob to this appointment.

Finally, Mark persuades Bob (while he is there) to 'self-exclude' himself from the site where he lost his money, and to call his relatives to stay with him for the next 2 days. This will help him to manage his behaviour, until the priory session at least.

11am:

At 11am, Mark has a meeting with a 48 year old recovering alcoholic, named Joe. Mark has been working with Joe for approximately 3 months now, since he was released from prison. At times, this has been an emotionally difficult process. Joe turned to alcohol after losing his wife to an illness, and has been in and out of prison for the past 3 years. One of Mark's central aims when taking the case was to help Joe move on from the loss of his wife, and learn how to deal with his grief.

Today, Mark is meeting with Joe for an hour, to discuss recent developments. After a relapse two months ago, Joe seems to have turned his life around and is currently interviewing for a number of IT based jobs. He has not touched an alcoholic drink for the past 9 weeks. The purpose of the meeting today is primarily to work on how Joe can improve his chances of getting a job.

To aid this endeavour, Joe recently attended an appointment with a careers advisor – who specialises in improving interview techniques. Joe was really pleased with how this went, and felt that it had provided him with invaluable advice moving forward. He has 2 interviews in the next week, and feels much more confident going forward.

Mark also wants to discuss how Joe's counselling sessions, and alcoholic support meetings are going. Joe is full of praise for the latter, but remains sceptical about the former. He believes that he needs more extensive behavioural therapy, rather than simply discussing his issues. Mark agrees to look into this for him.

12pm:

At 12pm, Mark heads back to his office to have his lunch, and to write up reports on the previous two meetings. As he explains, this is a regular and very important part of his job description:

'It's important to file reports for every meeting that you have with clients. This allows you to log information, and come back to it if necessary. When you are dealing with large amounts of cases, this can be really useful. The information can also be used when submitting evidence or giving recommendations at hearings. As a Probation Officer, it is essential that you can call upon the past, in order to change the outlook of the future.'

2pm:

At 2pm, Mark has an appointment with another of his parolees. The individual in question is a 33 year old woman, who has recently been provided with housing by her local council. Mark has been handed £200 in cash, to help the woman purchase essential household items, such as a kettle, cutlery, a cooker and toiletries. Mark enjoys this, as it provides him with a chance to catch up on how the woman is getting on, in a less formal environment.

The individual in question is considered a 'low risk' offender on Mark's list. She was imprisoned for a short period of time for petty crimes related to stealing, and served out her sentence without any issues. Mark's only concern is how she will handle paying the bills for her new accommodation. In order to help her do this, Mark has booked her an appointment to see the same careers advisor as Joe.

During their shopping trip, the woman discusses her expectations for this and informs Mark what steps she has been taking to try and secure herself a job. Mark is slightly concerned that the woman is not doing enough to help herself at the moment, and believes she should be spending more time than she currently is looking for jobs. Following their shopping trip, Mark helps the woman bring her purchases back to the flat. He arranges a follow up appointment for 2 weeks' time.

3:30pm:

At 3:30pm, Mark returns to his office. Unfortunately, when he arrives, there is a woman at his desk waiting to see him. The woman is holding her 3 year old child, who is hysterical. After calming both mother and child down, Mark discovers that the woman is the partner of one of Mark's clients, Keith. Keith is currently on parole, after being imprisoned for domestic abuse. The woman claims that Keith punched her, and shows Mark a bruise on the left side of her cheek to prove it.

Mark is extremely disappointed by this, as he believed that Keith was making progress. He now has to begin the recall process, in order for Keith to return to prison.

4:30pm:

Mark's final appointment involves attending a parole hearing for one of his clients. Mark has been working with the client since he was released on parole 3 months ago, but unfortunately the individual has fallen back into old habits. Thus, Mark was forced to start the prison recall process. The offender has appealed and is now appearing before a parole board, to discuss the sentence. Mark is acting as a witness at the parole hearing. As he explains, this is one of the hardest parts of the job:

'It's hard to feel like you aren't betraying them, to some extent. You've built up a relationship with this person, and now you are standing up in front of a parole board and recommending that they

return to prison. You just have to remember that your primary duty of care is towards the public, even if that means placing an offender back in custody.'

The parole hearing ends with the client's appeal being rejected, and he is returned to custody on a standard recall. As the offender leaves the room, he gestures obscenely to Mark. While this is upsetting, it reinforces Mark's view that he has done the right thing.

5:30pm:

At 5:30pm, Mark returns to the office to finish filing reports, replying to emails and updating his diary for the next day.

GEMMA'S DAY

6am:

Gemma's day begins at 6am. The first thing she does is visit the gym. She does 45 minutes of exercise, pops home for a shower and then heads off to the office. As she explains, physical and mental well-being are extremely important in this role:

'It's really important to stay fit and healthy. The healthier you are physically, the healthier you will be mentally. If you aren't in the right mental state of mind then you will really struggle to perform this job competently. I try to visit the gym at least 3 times a week.'

7:30am:

Gemma arrives at the office at half past 7. The first thing she does is to check her emails and appointment book. As Gemma is fairly new to the role (having worked there for 2 years), she is currently taking exterior courses to try and aid her development. One of her emails this morning is from a course provider, confirming her place. This course is due to take place tomorrow. For the next hour, Gemma re-arranges her daily priorities and makes phone calls in accordance with this. She has a number of high priority changes to make, and as a result will need to see different people to whom she was expecting, As she explains, this is one of the biggest challenges of the job:

'When most people go into work, they have a set plan of what they'll do that day. I do too, but very often that plan changes. Offenders are unpredictable and will challenge you in ways that you never expect. It gets easier with experience, but as someone who has only been doing this for 2 years, I'm constantly surprised by the way that things can change on such an immediate basis.'

Just before she is about to head out, Gemma receives a particularly distressing phone call from one of her clients. She immediately places this as her number one priority.

8:30am:

At 8:30am, Gemma makes her way to her first appointment. The client in question has been on parole for 2 months now (after stealing) and seemed to be making good progress. Unfortunately Gemma has received a phone call from the client, who works at a local shop, informing her that she needs help immediately.

When Gemma arrives at the scene, the individual is sitting outside on the pavement, smoking. He has been crying and informs Gemma that he has been having urges to steal from his employer, and that he rang Gemma because he fears that he is going to make a huge mistake. Gemma consoles the man, but tells him in no uncertain terms that if he is to act upon his urges, she will have to begin the recall process. The individual in question has already been to various behavioural therapy sessions to treat what has been diagnosed as Kleptomania. Despite this, he has still managed to get himself a job and held down the position for over a month now, in an environment where his disorder could prove extremely damaging.

After chatting with the man, Gemma promises him that she will organise a follow up visit with his psychiatrist for later that afternoon. If he continues to have urges, she advises him to go home immediately. The man seems contented with this solution, for now. As Gemma explains, situations like this are extremely difficult:

'While I'm there to support offenders and try to help them fix their issues, ultimately you are the only person who can change the way you behave. In a scenario such as the above, the only thing I can really do is support and advise. I can't physically stop the offender from stealing, but if he did then I'd have to take immediate action. It's difficult having to separate yourself in this way.'

9:30am:

Gemma's next appointment is at her local prison, with an offender who has recently been placed back into custody. Gemma was forced to begin the recall process after the offender was physically abusive towards his wife (which he was originally incarcerated for).

Since Gemma spoke negatively about the offender at the parole hearing, the pair have not had a cooperative relationship. The offender is rude and disrespectful towards Gemma, and refuses to acknowledge her authority. He blames her for the fact that he is back in prison, and claims that she betrayed his trust.

On this occasion, Gemma has received an email from one of the prison staff, claiming that the individual has been causing trouble for other prisoners. When Gemma arrives to visit the man, he is again rude and disrespectful. He claims that he won't take advice from a woman, and makes inappropriate comments. As Gemma explains, this is something that she has learned to manage:

'Sexism isn't acceptable in any form of environment, but in an environment such as mine, it's to be expected that certain individuals will try to use my gender against me. What you have to remember is that they are only damaging themselves. If they won't cooperate, they have less chance of being released. The key is to show them

that you aren't intimidated, and that your gender doesn't make a difference to how well you can do the job.'

Unfortunately on this occasion the offender refuses to acknowledge Gemma, and continues to make inappropriate comments. After trying to negotiate with him, Gemma simply asks him to leave the room.

11am:

At 11am, Gemma returns to the office to fill in the paperwork from the previous two cases, and to answer outstanding recommendations and forms. As soon as she sits down, she receives a phone call from her local Magistrate Court, informing her that one of her clients has been arrested and charged with aggravated assault and burglary.

Thus, as well as breaking the law anyway, he is in breach of his probationary terms. Gemma is aware that there are also child protection concerns regarding the individual, which puts her on red alert. She immediately makes the decision that the offender should be recalled into custody. Following this, she needs to submit the correct paperwork. This delays her by over an hour.

12pm:

At 12pm, Gemma has an introductory appointment with a new client. The client in question has just been released from prison, and is looking to get his life back on track. Gemma sits down with the individual to discuss what he would like to achieve whilst working with her, his previous criminal history and what steps he has already taken to amend himself. Together they produce a plan of positive action, and agree to meet again in 2 weeks' time.

1pm:

At 1pm, just as Gemma is about to sit down and eat her lunch, she receives a phone call from one of her clients. The client is threatening to kill himself. This is the fourth time in the last few weeks that he has done this, but Gemma is extremely concerned. She encourages him to make contact with the Samaritans, and gives him the number. After hanging up, she also calls the local police so that they can conduct a routine welfare check on the individual.

2pm:

At 2pm, Gemma attends a probationary hearing for one of her clients. On this occasion, Gemma actually speaks in favour of the client. The individual in question was recently caught up in a fight at a local establishment, thereby breaking the terms of his parole. However, Gemma has information that indicates that the individual was not involved in the fight. She recommends to the board that the individual be given leeway, and indicates that his behaviour since release is exemplary. Based on this information, the board decide to accept the defendants appeal. Gemma is thrilled with this outcome:

'My primary duty of care is to the public; and that means rehabilitating offenders so that they won't re-offend. If I genuinely believe that an offender shouldn't be placed back in custody, I'll say so. The board won't always accept my recommendations but my authority is given a fairly large weight.'

3pm:

At 3pm, Gemma returns to her office for a pre-sentence report interview, with a new client. This is the first time that she has met the client, who is dressed in a suit and tie. After getting all of the background on the case, and interviewing the man, Gemma writes a letter recommending that he receives community service as a penalty for his actions.

4pm:

For the final hour of her day, Gemma finishes writing reports, recommendations and emails. This includes:

- Writing a letter to a client's GP, as she is concerned about his emotional wellbeing;

- Completing a letter of recommendation for a client who has been banned from driving;

- Calling a social worker in regards to a child support case that she is extremely concerned about.

CHAPTER 8

A Few Final Words

You have now reached the end of this guide and no doubt will be ready to start preparing for the Probation Officer selection process.

The majority of candidates who pass the selection process have a number of common attributes. These are as follows:

1. They believe in themselves.

The first factor is self-belief. Regardless of what anyone tells you, you can become a Probation Officer. Just like any job, you have to be prepared to work hard in order to be successful. Make sure that you have the self-belief to pass the selection process and fill your mind with positive thoughts.

2. They prepare fully.

The second factor is preparation. Those people who achieve in life prepare fully for every eventuality, and that is what you must do when you apply to become a Probation Officer. Work hard, and concentrate on improving your weakest areas.

3. They persevere.

Everybody comes across obstacles or setbacks in their life, but it is what you do about those setbacks that is important. If you fail at something, then ask yourself 'why' you have failed. This will allow you to improve for next time. If you keep improving and trying, success will follow.

4. They are self-motivated.

How much do you want this job? Do you want it, or do you *really* want it? When you apply to join the probation service, you should want it more than anything in the world. During the weeks and months leading up to the probation selection process, keep yourself motivated, eat healthy and maintain your fitness levels.

Work hard, stay focused and you can achieve anything that you set your mind to.